UNDERSTANDING
DON DELILLO

UNDERSTANDING CONTEMPORARY AMERICAN LITERATURE

Matthew J. Bruccoli, Founding Editor

Linda Wagner-Martin, Series Editor

Volumes on

Edward Albee | Sherman Alexie | Nelson Algren
Paul Auster | Nicholson Baker | John Barth | Donald Barthelme
The Beats | Thomas Berger | The Black Mountain Poets
Robert Bly | T. C. Boyle | Truman Capote | Raymond Carver
Michael Chabon | Fred Chappell | Chicano Literature
Contemporary American Drama | Contemporary American Horror Fiction
Contemporary American Literary Theory
Contemporary American Science Fiction, 1926–1970
Contemporary American Science Fiction, 1970–2000
Contemporary Chicana Literature | Robert Coover | Don DeLillo
Philip K. Dick | James Dickey | E. L. Doctorow | Rita Dove | Dave Eggers
John Gardner | George Garrett | Tim Gautreaux | John Hawkes
Joseph Heller | Lillian Hellman | Beth Henley | James Leo Herlihy
David Henry Hwang | John Irving | Randall Jarrell | Charles Johnson
Diane Johnson | Adrienne Kennedy | William Kennedy | Jack Kerouac
Jamaica Kincaid | Etheridge Knight | Tony Kushner | Ursula K. Le Guin
Denise Levertov | Bernard Malamud | David Mamet | Bobbie Ann Mason
Colum McCann | Cormac McCarthy | Jill McCorkle | Carson McCullers
W. S. Merwin | Arthur Miller | Steven Millhauser | Lorrie Moore
Toni Morrison's Fiction | Vladimir Nabokov | Gloria Naylor
Joyce Carol Oates | Tim O'Brien | Flannery O'Connor | Cynthia Ozick
Suzan-Lori Parks | Walker Percy | Katherine Anne Porter | Richard Powers
Reynolds Price | Annie Proulx | Thomas Pynchon | Theodore Roethke
Philip Roth | Richard Russo | May Sarton | Hubert Selby, Jr.
Mary Lee Settle | Sam Shepard | Neil Simon | Isaac Bashevis Singer
Jane Smiley | Gary Snyder | William Stafford | Robert Stone | Anne Tyler
Gerald Vizenor | Kurt Vonnegut | David Foster Wallace | Robert Penn
Warren | James Welch | Eudora Welty | Colson Whitehead
Tennessee Williams | August Wilson | Charles Wright

UNDERSTANDING
DON DELILLO

Henry Veggian

The University of South Carolina Press

Published by the University of South Carolina Press
Columbia, South Carolina 29208

uscpress.com

Printed in the United States of America

Library of Congress Cataloging-in-Publication Data
can be found at http://catalog.loc.gov/.

CONTENTS

SERIES EDITOR'S PREFACE

The Understanding Contemporary American Literature series was founded by the estimable Matthew J. Bruccoli (1931–2008), who envisioned these volumes as guides or companions for students as well as good nonacademic readers, a legacy that will continue as new volumes are developed to fill in gaps among the nearly one hundred series volumes published to date and to embrace a host of new writers only now making their marks on our literature.

As Professor Bruccoli explained in his preface to the volumes he edited, because much influential contemporary literature makes special demands, "the word understanding in the titles was chosen deliberately. Many willing readers lack an adequate understanding of how contemporary literature works; that is, of what the author is attempting to express and the means by which it is conveyed." Aimed at fostering this understanding of good literature and good writers, the criticism and analysis in the series provide instruction in how to read certain contemporary writers—explicating their material, language, structures, themes, and perspectives—and facilitate a more profitable experience of the works under discussion.

In the twenty-first century Professor Bruccoli's prescience gives us an avenue to publish expert critiques of significant contemporary American writing. The series continues to map the literary landscape and to provide both instruction and enjoyment. Future volumes will seek to introduce new voices alongside canonized favorites, to chronicle the changing literature of our times, and to remain, as Professor Bruccoli conceived, contemporary in the best sense of the word.

Linda Wagner-Martin, Series Editor

PREFACE

Raised by the newspaper and the broadsheet, the pamphlet and the poem, the first American novelists were bound to the print culture of the late eighteenth century. Who can read Charles Brockden Brown or Susanna Haswell Rowson and not be reminded that Philadelphia, the young nation's first great cultural center, was perched at the edge of a boundless forest whose mineral resources a royal decree had once prevented from being made into a printing press? And even after the fact, when a press was eventually permitted in Philadelphia, it was entrusted only to a Royalist named William Bradford, a man whose son was also a printer and later a rival to Benjamin Franklin. If Poor Richard freely gave advice, his type had come at no small risk or cost, as Franklin was forced to sail to England to purchase the machinery required to make books. Memory of the precarious and adversarial circumstances of the colonial press lingered until after the American War of Independence, and it underscores the cautionary tones of post-Revolutionary writers such as Brown and Rowson. Novelists suspected that should the public stop reading, a print culture won by the pen would be reclaimed by the sword.

The republic's young novelists quickly encountered another and perhaps unexpected difficulty: a crowded literary market. Rowson confirms as much when in the preface to *Charlotte Temple: A Tale of Truth* (1794) she describes her awareness of being "a novel writer, at a time when such a variety of works are ushered into the world under that name." Several decades would pass before the American literary novel would earn lasting critical prestige and a place at the fore of the cultural imaginary. In contrast to its precarious youth, the American novel's history is so pervasive today that towns and cities have nearly become synonymous with certain novelists: Salem, Massachusetts; Hannibal, Missouri; Oxford, Mississippi; Salinas, California. The American novel also travels well: when Thomas Pynchon sets the majority of *Gravity's Rainbow* (1973) in post–World War II Europe, we do not hesitate to call it an American novel. Conversely, when writers from other national traditions find success in the United States, we welcome their fiction with open arms. Nabokov, Pasternak, Lampedusa, Marquez, Lessing, Coetzee, Saramago, and

Pahmuk all recently enjoyed large readerships in America. When a novelist accused of having written a novel flees from persecution and death for having written it, as was the case for Solzhenitsyn and Rushdie, we provide them sanctuary, and we have done so despite (and perhaps to stir) the diplomatic trouble that such hospitality may entail. Even when much has changed, American readers and writers carry to this day a strong vestigial memory of the admonition and doubt that troubled our early novelists. We remember that a national literature must be defended; we remember how the rosebush concluding the first chapter of *The Scarlet Letter* blooms beside a prison.

We have also arrived at a time when influential critics and commentators acknowledge a decline in the novel's cultural influence and prestige. Jonathan Arac described the matter in a 2009 essay when discussing Chang Rae Lee's novel *Native Speaker* (1995): "I find the novel now a residual form, no longer dominant as it had once seemed some fifty years ago." Arac nonetheless affirms that "the residual practice of the novel performs at least one essential cultural task. The novel stands up for the human, in an age that seems to find even more ways to erode humanity."[1] Arac denotes a specific century—from roughly 1850 to 1950—to mark the perimeter and depth of the novel's ferment in the United States and beyond it. One would not dispute that countless readers across the world currently enjoy the labors of novelists and their publishers. Nonetheless there is considerable merit to the claim that the novel is closing a particularly American phase of its history, and not only in America. The possible causes are many. One might say the novel no longer satisfies the ambitions of a nation's youth as it did during the Jazz Age, for the Popular Front, for veterans attending college on the G.I. Bill, or for the Beat generation. Nor is it the surrogate field upon which ideologies waged proxy battles during the Cold War. Blame computers if you will. Managed to respectability, the novel may no longer seem a daring form. That is to say it no longer seems daring if one finds human life, memory, politics, language, history, science, art, emotion, experience, or work to be unremarkable.

Don DeLillo is known primarily for the novels he has produced over the course of a writing career that now spans more than fifty years. Beginning with his first published story in 1960 (his first novel was published in 1971), he has written and regularly published literary fiction during the period of the modern American novel's alleged decline. DeLillo has often visited the question of the novel's status in his fiction and addressed the matter in interviews. He noted in a 1993 interview with Adam Begley: "The novel's not dead, it's not even seriously injured, but I do think we're working at the margins, working in the shadow of the novel's greatness and influence. There's plenty of impressive talent around, and there's strong evidence that younger writers are moving into history, finding broader themes. But when we talk about the novel we have to consider the culture in which it operates. Everything in the culture argues against the novel, particularly the novel that tries to be equal to the complexities and excesses of the culture."[2] DeLillo proceeds to name William Gaddis, Thomas Pynchon, Joan Didion, Cormac McCarthy, Robert Coover, Robert Stone, and other novelists as examples of the novel's contemporary vitality, and then qualifies his point: "These books and writers show us that the novel is still spacious enough and brave enough to encompass enormous areas of experience. We have a rich literature. But sometimes it's a literature too ready to be neutralized, to be incorporated into the ambient noise. This is why we need the writer in opposition, the novelist who writes against power, who writes against the corporation or the state or the whole apparatus of assimilation."[3] The latter comment would seem to align DeLillo with the oppositional spirit of the 1960s (and while he is not a baby boomer, the affiliation may stand). Considered more broadly, DeLillo's comments on the novel's status as a literary form remind us of that centuries-old habit of the American literary imaginary to regard literature as vulnerable, marginal, and besieged by monarchs or markets.

DeLillo's comments on the novel's status also dispel the frequently encountered notion that DeLillo is in some way an aloof, difficult, and pessimistic writer. Yes, his writing requires the reader's commitment and intelligence. What art does not? Yes, he is reserved in conversation, particularly during interviews. Who is not uncomfortable when asked to speak of themselves in public? Surely, his novels do not offer generic satisfactions. Do we remember and praise great art for its predictability? If we dismiss these inherited notions of "difficult art" or caricatures of the writer as a mythic recluse, we might begin to regard DeLillo as an artist who consciously and carefully occupies a particular band along the wavelength of the modern literary novel, along which his interviews, fiction, and career often express a gregarious and forward-looking sense of the novel's role and history. It is a sense grounded in the complexities of the present time; rather than offering utopian alternatives or dystopian scenarios, DeLillo works like the artist Klara Sax in his 1997 novel *Underworld,* making literary art—"found art"—from contemporary life. He works through culture, language, and the novel to dramatize, as Peter Knight has described it, "the problematic role of the artist in an age of boundless consumerism."[4] One would not call it a hopeful literature, but to call it hopeless would also be unfair.

One might instead look to DeLillo's career as it embodies "the writer in opposition" and recognize in it strong evidence that the novel is instead passing through an exciting phase in both its American and worldly history. In this view, Don DeLillo's writing career affirms the art of the novel in the present time (and by implication, as a democratic institution with an individual as well as historical range). In a very important sense, his fiction and career dramatize the current plight of the novel as an art form as well as the general state of the artist and the arts. While that drama can seem tragic at times, it is never without comedy or optimism. For Don DeLillo the novel is a popular art form, what Bill Gray describes in *Mao II* as a "democratic shout" (159). When novelists write, they elaborate a vernacular truth against which propaganda, the demagogue, and the state cannot stand for long. This political view of DeLillo's fiction has recently become a strong current in conversations about his work, and it is one of several views that appear in this book.

When I write that Don DeLillo is an *American* writer, I invite the reader to consider the triple significance of the phrase. First, DeLillo's novels frequently assume the reader's familiarity with history (if only to then make it strangely unfamiliar). The effect might be compared to visiting one's birthplace after a long absence: we recognize it but something intangible has nonetheless changed. For example, the armored stretch limousine of a young financial wizard named Eric Packer navigates antiglobalization riots in the streets of New York City in DeLillo's novel *Cosmopolis* (2003). The president of the United States is visiting the city, his motorcade blocking traffic. Everything in the novel seems contemporary with the presidency of William Jefferson Clinton, the financial "dot-com" crash of the late 1990s, and the antiglobalization protests that marked the turn of the century. Yet the president's name is not Clinton (it is Midwood), and the rioters have adopted slogans and symbols that have no direct equivalent in history or the news. As a result, New York City itself assumes an otherworldly atmosphere. Is this an America parallel to our own, a place into which we cross in those rare moments when we let down our guard, dream, or read? The effect is as true for DeLillo's Texas (a setting in several of his novels) as it is for DeLillo's New York. In this sense of the phrase "American writer," I assume that readers will recognize names, persons, places, terms, and events that shaped the twentieth century and also the young millennium, but also recognize them as occupying a narrative space on this side of DeLillo's novels. If we understand the simple but powerful role that adjectives can play in transforming a noun, then it is a first step to understanding the care with which DeLillo uses words in his literary fiction and a first step across the threshold of his novels.

Conversely, the noun in the phrase "American writer" inflects the adjective. DeLillo seemingly holds to the belief that art and artists, and novelists in particular, play an important role in shaping the republic of the United States of America. DeLillo's depiction of artists and his own public appearances underscore this belief. The latter do not resemble conventional book-tour "readings" so much as artistic performances. (Their somber, meditative intonations offer something unlike a conventional spectacle.) DeLillo will read fiction at public appearances, most often a work whose relationship to the occasion seems circumspect, even suspicious, but which over time appears relevant, forceful, and even cathartic. I have attended these readings on several occasions over the course of three decades, and they never cease to surprise. He reads at a library for a gathering in defense of human rights, on the occasion of a friend's retirement, at a memorial service for a fellow writer, in a school or theater or the hall of a YMCA building. These appearances embody a determined loyalty to the ideal of what the role of public art in a republic can and might be, an ideal that takes a tangible, physical form as art moving through public spaces, individuals, and crowds. Many readers cling to a false notion that DeLillo is a sort of hermit, aloof and remote. He is certainly a private, guarded individual, but as noted above, it may be more useful to recognize in the democratic spirit of his public literary interventions and published works the thoughtful, artful performances of an "American *writer.*" In this second sense, the public connotations of the noun complicate the adjective in unexpected ways. It also may serve to help readers appreciate the artists who appear as characters in much of his fiction.

There is a third sense of "American writer" that I ask the reader to entertain. It places the phrase along a historical spectrum. At one end there is the marketplace; at the other, the institution of the novel as one cornerstone of the American's writer's craft. As for the market, in a series of brilliant essays and books that he published in the 1940s and 1950s, the Ohio State University professor William Charvat documented how "authorship" became a respected practice in the nineteenth-century United States. In material terms that profession stimulated a new scale for affiliated industries (publishing houses, periodicals, and the papermaking, printing, and binding manufactories, not to mention retailers such as stationers and booksellers). In demographic and cultural terms, the new economy of the American writer amplified the instruction and entertainment of an ever-widening audience of readers. Beginning with the New York writers of the Hudson Valley (Irving, Paulding, Cooper) and extending through the New England of Longfellow, Fuller, Hawthorne, Melville, Emerson, and Thoreau (with Poe as a critical southern outlier), Charvat uses empirical evidence such as publisher's ledgers, advertisements, and other historical sources to describe, as the title of one of his posthumously published books calls it, *The Profession of Authorship in America, 1800–1870*. Economics and literary business in general is a recurrent theme in DeLillo's novels. While writing this book, I found it useful to consider DeLillo's career in terms of how his writings have engaged, commented upon, and depicted what it meant to be a writer when he began his career in the age of mass media and printed books, as well as today in an age when the old print media have welcomed a digital sibling. I believe that view illuminates DeLillo's career as well as his writings about mass media or the role of the artist in society. In one sense this view also asks readers to consider DeLillo's own iteration of that playful postmodern habit of writing books that frustrate readers and resist easy commodification, thereby clarifying to some degree DeLillo's phrase about "the writer in opposition."

At the other end of that spectrum, DeLillo's writings also belong to the tradition of the modern novel and the American novel within that tradition. The "institution of the novel" is a phrase with a rich and varied history, but it is first and foremost a metaphor that signals the literary novel's uncanny capacity for shaping and inventing reality (and vice versa). Simultaneous with Charvat's studies, mid-twentieth-century American intellectuals, and particularly the Harvard scholar Harry Levin, proposed another story of how the institution of the novel took its American form during the nineteenth century. In the version of literary history told by intellectuals who later elaborated Levin's argument, the novel attained a privileged position in American culture. (We hear a version of that argument in the above quotations from Jonathan Arac.) In their view, the novel's unique generative properties brought a national culture into existence. In this sense the "institution" of the novel was not only the effect of material causes (for example, the rise of industries and readerships), but it was also a cause of material effects (the rise of industries and readerships). In generating a national culture, the American novel also conversed with other national literary traditions. From the romances of the Scottish writer Sir Walter Scott, Cooper found a model for telling the story of the American frontier. In the French realists of the nineteenth century, Hawthorne recognized a certain kinship for his contemporary novels. For mid-twentieth-century writers (including DeLillo) who read Kafka, Joyce, Woolf, and Camus, modern European literatures offered new possibilities for writing American fiction after the Second World War. In English we translate Goethe's term *Weltliteratur* as "World Literature" and often understand the first word to be an adjective. In the German, however, both words are nouns, things that are conjoined. In the institutional view of the novel, America and the novel have enjoyed a similar relationship.

America, the novel, the novelist, and the world: they are the works of readers and writers. In American history we came to privilege the writer, and particularly the novelist, and we continue that tradition to this day. We privilege those writers because we regard them as biographers of the republic's early years. We think of novelists as reflecting that biography in a miniature form, from the "early" writings of Rowson and Brown, Paulding, Irving, and Cooper, to a metaphorical maturity that begins with Hawthorne and Melville and continues through James and Wharton, Fitzgerald, Faulkner, and Hemingway, and finally to the present time. If we follow the biographical conceit, we may think that we have arrived at the national equivalent of what Edward W. Said defined as a "late style." But is that late style typified by what he calls "wise resignation" or that of "a renewed, almost youthful energy?"[5] The former sense is that by which some regard the phrase "American writer" in the present time, as a phrase suggesting a republic's venerable senescence: the novel as an institution in ruin, its pieces like stones fallen about a temple in a Romantic painting. Some even regard DeLillo in this way, as a writer past his prime.

I admit that DeLillo's career took an entirely unexpected turn since we entered the new century, and one that might resemble the taciturn grumpiness that Said described so well in his study of the late works of Ibsen, Lampedusa, Mann, and Genet. But I would point also to a renewed sense of innovation in DeLillo's recent fiction, a heightened sense of the beautiful to match the incomparable terrors that were a trademark of his twentieth-century works. This book tries to strike a balance between the two, but when writing about DeLillo as an American writer, I have avoided the temptation to suggest that DeLillo's recent work is in some way indicative of a decline. The notion is utterly false so far as I am concerned, and it does not apply to DeLillo or other talented writers working in the present day, be they young or old. My stated position does not appeal to any vapid patriotism or exceptionalism with respect to the American novel's status. It appeals instead to a philosophical premise that DeLillo's fiction shares with much of the critical writing about it, not to mention common sense: it is the philosophical notion that we are sure to be wrong when we bracket history and prophesy to declare its end. More important, in doing so we would thereby obstruct that line of creative flight along which we may encounter what we may yet become—if it is not already too late.

But there is also a more practical reason why I avoid the bleakest connotations of "late style" insofar as the phrase would draw a relationship between DeLillo's career and the decline of the American novel. It is because regardless of the framework we use to explain it, DeLillo's career and his novels do not fit in any neat way into the narratives we tell about the American novel. One might say this of any important novelist, but DeLillo's writings of the twenty-first century openly defy the notion that novelists have exhausted the aesthetic potential of the form in which they work, and furthermore his recent achievements refute the idea that the novel has entered a historical twilight (in America or elsewhere). It is impossible to ignore the differences in character, rhetoric, narration, mood, or timing when comparing DeLillo's twentieth-century writings to those of the twenty-first century. As a result, their biographies are simply not continuous. At times the developmental arc of DeLillo's fiction, working from his earliest novels to the most recent, nearly seems the work of two different writers.

This book is organized to reflect this notion in some way, but also to trace lines of continuity that will help the reader appreciate DeLillo's literary fiction. In sum, this is a book about a novelist who makes a strong case for the institution of the novel as a form of symbolic communication in the world—an "American writer" and all that the phrase might and does entail.

ACKNOWLEDGMENTS

I am grateful to Linda Wagner-Martin for offering the opportunity to write this volume. Jim Denton, Linda Fogle, Patricia Callahan, Bill Adams, and the staff of the University of South Carolina Press provided exemplary editorial advice. I thank them for their work in cultivating and completing the project. Rosemary Morrow of Redux Pictures was resourceful and patient in finding and arranging the use of the cover photograph, and I am grateful to her for her work. I owe particular thanks to Professor Daniel Bronson of Montclair State University for introducing me to the writings of Don DeLillo many years ago. I thank Fan Xiaomei for bringing the translated Chinese editions of DeLillo's novels to my attention. Friends, students, and colleagues who were gracious in offering perspective and dialogue for which I owe thanks include Bradley Fest, Doreen Michleski, Jennifer Larson, Richard Purcell, Thomas Reinert, Christopher McKenna, Florence Dore, and Scott Dill. To my parents, Pia and Dino, and my children, Leo and Josie, I am forever thankful.

CHAPTER 1

Understanding Don DeLillo

Criticism and Biography

When literary critics refer to "authorship" today, the term no longer carries with it the assumption of a personal "style." I refer here to the argument that a literary work such as a novel or poem communicates a writer's biography, intentions, or selfhood in any transparent manner to the reader. The matter applies to the most impersonal writers as well as the most confessional and autobiographical. DeLillo would seem to belong with the former group of writers whose literature appears immune to biographical interpretation. Furthermore, in interviews he has consistently evaded extensive commentary on his own life and also avoided writing about his own life in any explicit way, in fiction or elsewhere. It would seem that both DeLillo and some of his more influential readers and critics, the latter group reinforced by the tremendously influential twentieth-century theories of language, mind, and literature that reconfigured all our assumptions about how we can experience art, have obstructed possible discussions of DeLillo's biography. This is not to suggest they conspired to do so: it simply works out that DeLillo's fiction does not explicitly disclose personal information about the writer's life. Curiously, however, DeLillo writes often *about* biography (if not his own). In addition, critical studies of DeLillo's career often contain important observations on the relationship between his life, career, and art, observations that would seem to contradict the premise of much critical writing about DeLillo. It is a curious, and rather productive, series of contradictions.

Contemporary critics begin from the position that the study of literature cannot presume any easy relationship between the artist's life and the art. Some take this position as the starting point for a discussion of the cultural forces that shape literary works; literature, they argue, is to be read as a "social text," something determined by forces a writer cannot control: class, race, gender, language, and so on. Literature becomes in this view a catch basin into which language is diverted by external social forces. There is little if any agency afforded to the writer in such treatments of literature, wherein the work is generally regarded as a sort of passive commodity that suddenly appears as the result of predetermined social pressures. In another, less current view, we might still regard the literary work as an artifact also without any relation to the author's life or experience, and one whose relationship to that life is furthermore immaterial. In this view, we study literature according to certain rules that govern the evaluation of literary works. What are its rhetorical properties? Is it ironic? Paradoxical? Is it a generic work? How so? Where might it be categorized? Literature is thus severed from biography and history, these being modes of reading that formal literary analysis regards as extraneous to literary experience. While both views have their legitimate scientific models and merits, both also eliminate biography or reduce it to the status of an unwelcome guest in the house of literary criticism and cultural analysis.

It does not require much thought to admit that these views defy the laws of physics. A writer must sit down somewhere and write for hours and days and weeks and even years. In doing so, he or she chooses words and assembles literary artifice, labors through genres, modes, and styles, reflects (or deflects) personal predilections and takes positions with respect to widely recognized traditions and debates. Biographical criticism therefore works from the reasonable assumption that there exists a significant relationship between a writer's life and the writer's art. Rather than view the writer as an unwelcome guest in the house of criticism, the literary biographer views the writer as a reluctant host. Critics visit, eat the appetizers, and move on to ruin someone else's carpets. The biographer stays behind trying to coax the writer's life out from a room that it refuses to leave. The writer may very well become available, but the life is always somewhere else.

And so while the great modern theories and critics have made the literary art of biography a rather difficult one, there may also be opportunity for it in that chaos. After all, longing for prior modes of expression is widely accepted as a defining feature of postmodern literature such as that written by DeLillo. Who is to say that the art of biography is not the expression of a postmodern longing to describe a "life," even if that previous notion of individual life (the romantic hero, the fragmented modern subject, and so forth) was itself a myth—and a useful one at that? A postmodern biography of DeLillo's life and career would require accounting in some way for the artifice of biography.

For example, it might very well resemble what DeLillo composed when he wrote *Libra* (1988), a novel depicting the "life" of Lee Harvey Oswald. After one reads *Libra* it is difficult to avoid noticing DeLillo's career-long habit of depicting characters who are concerned with recounting the lives of others or even setting out to recount their own lives. (For example, the latter is the central dilemma of DeLillo's first novel, *Americana,* published in 1971.) Understood in this way, the writing of a fictional biography (or obituary, or fictional interview about an artist's work) appears as an evasive, difficult, yet entirely worthwhile endeavor insofar as DeLillo treats it as a literary genre rather than as a statement of fact designed to reduce art to the evidence or alleged facts of a life.

For the present purpose it is necessary simply to acknowledge that DeLillo often writes from the intersection where life and fiction collide. Granted that life is not his own, but reading the sections of *Libra* that are set in DeLillo's childhood neighborhood in the Bronx, one cannot help but sense a certain sympathy between writer and milieu. I would borrow from an early work by the late Edward W. Said to explain briefly that effect in a manner that does not reduce a novel to biography but rather sustains a relationship between the two. In a shrewd book entitled *Joseph Conrad and the Fiction of Autobiography,* Said argued that Conrad's seafaring fictions were effective because their author diminished his own maritime experience in those writings, thereby making room for literary characterization and event. In Said's words, Conrad "*economized himself.*"[1] The relationship between DeLillo's fiction and life may be said to do the same. In addition, he has often admitted his debt to modernist narrative techniques (if not Conrad) that are circumspect regarding their authors' personal lives. (Joyce's fiction would seem significant in this respect.) More important, DeLillo's fiction often makes that same circumspection into the subject of a novel. The result is a literary fiction wherein characters or narrators dissolve into art. DeLillo's beautiful and moving short novel *The Body Artist* (2001) exemplifies the process. We might say that as DeLillo "economizes himself" by withholding autobiography from his fiction, his fiction does something more in that it makes self-effacement into literary art.

And so we are precluded by much of a century of argument that prohibits reconstructing life from art. Further still, even if such a thing were possible, it would be extremely difficult, if not impossible, to reverse engineer DeLillo's biography from his art, even if certain critics I will later mention have made persuasive cases for it. Readers can nonetheless keep in mind that life and biography play a constant role in his work even when the life or biography in question is not necessarily his own, or when a life is being artfully immersed in fiction rather than substantiated off the page.

One biographical fact about DeLillo has remained constant, however, through the clamor and debate: in interviews, readings, and public conversation, DeLillo prefers to discuss his art, and art in general, rather than his life. If an interviewer asks a question of a biographical nature, DeLillo may briefly entertain it only to direct his answer to other discussions of writing, art, and culture. This much can be said with certainty: DeLillo loves to discuss the relationship between art and life, but he does so at times by avoiding the very questions that would offer perspective on their relationship to his own life and art. If one were to write a biography of DeLillo based only upon DeLillo the public figure, his would appear to be a life thoroughly preoccupied with writing, art, and thoughtful consideration of the role of literature in the world. Regarded in this way, his career seems less enigmatic. Perhaps it would appear "selfless" in some other, more important or more substantive way.

The situation is complicated by the lack of verifiable "facts." Until recently the only information available about DeLillo's life came from his interviews or a scant public record. Over the past decade, however, the accumulation of interviews he has given, paired with the digitization and public dissemination of U.S. government records, provides a more thorough account. One cannot say it is comprehensive, or that one might say to the writer as the government operative says to Jack Gladney in *White Noise* (1985), that "you are the sum total of your data" (181). In addition to the available materials, a biography of DeLillo's life and career might even one day use DeLillo's papers and correspondence, which he recently gave to the archives of the Harry Ransom Center for the Humanities at the University of Texas at Austin. Transcripts, records, and archives do not, however, speak for themselves; rather, the biographer speaks through them, distorting or clarifying them in order to tell a story of a life. This process is complicated by the migration of facts to new technological platforms. For most of modern history, nameless clerks compiled forms, filed them, and kept the archives we refer to as "historical record." Today that information becomes the aforementioned "data," a metastatic body of information that is not so much kept as it is sorted, stored by, and accessed through powerful computer servers. On memorable occasions, as when Jack Gladney of *White Noise* learns from a computer of the statistical probability of his own death following a spill of toxic waste, DeLillo describes how we encounter and react to such things—in rather comical ways, in this case. It is also useful to approach the material in the way that the CIA archivist/historian Nicholas Branch considers the computerized archive of "facts" about Lee Harvey Oswald in DeLillo's 1988 novel *Libra:* with an eye for how information betrays patterns and connections. As is often the case in DeLillo's fiction, orders emerge from such patterns, orders that suggest other ways of apprehending a writer's life or work, but also in ways that may never amount to any absolute truth. Biography, in this sense, is a form of speculation that proceeds by a self-effacement comparable to that of DeLillo's most evasive characterizations.

Biography

Donald Richard DeLillo was born on November 20, 1936, in New York City. His parents were Italian immigrants. His paternal name, "DeLillo," is not uncommon in the Apennine Mountains that bisect the "boot" of Southern Italy. The Ellis Island passenger records of debarked immigrants list a total of forty-eight entries with the last name DeLillo between 1893 and 1922, the majority being from that region. Of those forty-eight names, two claimed the United States as residence (suggesting a return from a trip to Italy), and three others are unintelligible or list no place of origin. Of the forty-three remaining names, eighteen are from the town of Savignano, a small municipality in the Apennine range, to the north and west of the city of Avellino. Another ten names declare Grumo, presumably the Grumo in the province of Naples (there are at least four other Italian towns with the name, three of those in the south, one in the north). Nine towns (including Caivano, Montagano, Irsona, Matrice, Montecalo, Modugno, and Vitadazio) account for the fifteen remaining DeLillo names on the Ellis Island registers during that period. In sum, nearly one third of the Italian immigrants named DeLillo who came to the United States near or after the turn of the last century hailed from a small town (Savignano) located in the Apennine mountain range, and the rest emigrated from similar towns in the region. Emigration from these towns reflects a broader pattern: the immigrants departed in clusters. There are four entries from Savignano from 1900 to 1901, and five entries from there in 1906 alone.

In a 1991 interview Don DeLillo told the British journalist Gordon Burn that his family immigrated to the United States in 1916. There is, however, no entry for the name DeLillo in the Ellis Island rolls for that year.[2] But there are two names, those of Rocco and Nicola DeLillo, who emigrated from Modugno, a town close to the Adriatic city of Bari, in the year 1915. One of the immigrants is listed as being three years of age, the other thirty—likely a father and his son. No other persons by the name of DeLillo are recorded as having entered the United States during World War I (1914–1918). The decline in Italian emigration was a direct result of Italy's involvement in the war, during which time the young republic fought to drive the Habsburgs out from its northern provinces and finally unify the nation. The nation's fathers and sons were thus sent to war and therefore could not emigrate. For mothers, wives, children, and daughters who wanted to leave, there were also German U-Boats to consider.

Thus the official immigration record seems a dead end. Yet history never ends in DeLillo's fiction; a new path is sure to open at some point. We have a clue to it from DeLillo himself, and it is the matriarchal possibility noted above. In the same interview in which he provided the date 1916, DeLillo described his family's immigration to America as follows: "There was my grandmother, my father and his brothers and sisters. There was a total of about seven people, including a dwarf, and a child my grandmother picked up in Naples along the way."[3] Naples, on the Tyrrhenian Sea, is on the opposite coast from Bari. Rocco and Nicholas are thereby eliminated as likely ancestors. We can surmise that DeLillo's family likely boarded a ship from the port of Naples or passed through Naples in transit to the larger port of Genoa. More important, it also raises the possibility that his grandmother was a widow; if that is true, then she likely gave her maiden name, according to Italian custom. Perhaps the family crossed in 1916, after all, through the Rubicon of submarine death and against the American war machine that was moving in the other direction across the sea, ultimately to give a name we do not know. Another dead end.

In the 1980s DeLillo offered yet another account of his family history, this time to the Italian writer and literary critic Fernanda Pivano. In her book *Amici Scrittori: Quarant' Anni di Incontri e Scoperte con gli Autori Americani,* Pivano devotes a long section of one chapter to DeLillo. There she describes his telling of a more thorough account—possibly the most thorough one—of his family history. Here is my translation:

> I had seen DeLillo often but always in New York because he obstinately refused Piront's invitation to visit Naples. I slowly drew out an account of his father whom DeLillo had taken to Italy before he [his father] became ill. He accompanied his father to the village of Mongano, near Campobasso, in the Abruzzi. DeLillo told me: "It was a beautiful experience for him to revisit his hometown for the last time. He went to America in 1917, at the age of nine, and began working for a large insurance company. My mother was born in the same town, not only the same town, but the same house, at a distance of four years. I learned of it only when we visited, as my father had never told me. Of Italian, little had stayed with him. My education was entirely American, as was his: he quickly learned English, and grew up on the West Side of Manhattan, until he moved to the Bronx."[4]

If we look at a map, we find Montagano (not "Mongano," which is likely a misprint), a small town just north and east of the slightly larger town of Matrice in the province of Campobasso. If we return to our original list of DeLillos who emigrated to America, we find two names from the region on the Ellis Island rolls: a Giuseppe DeLillo from Matrice (a town near Montagano) arrived in America in 1898, and a Gennaro DeLillo arrived in America from Montagano in 1901. The dead ends, probabilities, and accumulated errors of fact (including those in DeLillo's accounts), all point to a likely point of origin: Montagano was the town from which his family emigrated. We have the probable "where." We also have probable distant relatives (Gennaro and Giuseppe). The persons and places do not, however, align with any year; like chronological glitches, when narrative time skips like the needle on a vinyl record in DeLillo's novel *Cosmopolis,* the names or persons in DeLillo's published family anecdotes do not precisely align in memory or time. We have possibilities that conform to a pattern of immigration history, but the most important narrative—the specific family story—largely evades us.

The two DeLillo quotations above are the most substantial he has given to interviewers. The first, with its matrilineal persistence and Faulknerian dwarf, suggests a fable. It is gregarious and unexpected, transforming the ordinary into something remarkable. The second suggests instead the delicate pathos of immigrant memory. Sixty years removed from experiences that are not his own (yet seemingly no less intimate), DeLillo abruptly shifts from the tender moment of a father's revelations and turns instead to the business of America. Conjoin the tone of the two quotes, and you have a glimpse of the dramatic moods of DeLillo's prose. The fragments of history are significant after all: the record speaks even as it skips. The ambiguity of technology (the misprint), impossible chronologies, errors of memory that conceal stories yet also result in new narrative possibilities, the elusive shape of mystery as a narrative form, historical patterns of movement and countermovement as individuals and peoples move around the world—these count among the most recognizable elements of DeLillo's fiction.

Don DeLillo was not a physical part of that immigration history. Rather, he was born into it as a New Yorker and raised the child of immigrants. The trail of his actual biography resumes, after his birth record, at the age of three with the sixteenth United States census. It does not resume in New York, as one might expect, but in southeastern Pennsylvania. Conducted in 1940 by the U.S. Department of Commerce Bureau of the Census, its information was collected then, as now, by seasonal employees knocking on the doors of American homes and asking a series of questions of those who answered. The responses were entered into a standardized form published by the U.S. Government Print Office. And so from sheet number twelve of the "Population Schedule" survey form conducted on April 15, 1940, by a census employee named James Golamis in the town of Pottsville City, Pennsylvania, we learn that DeLillo's mother opened the door.

The form itself lists the names of Peter, Lina, and Donald DeLillo, ages thirty-three, twenty-nine, and three, respectively. The parents, Lina and Peter, list their country of residence as Italy while young Donald is listed as a resident of New York. Peter is listed as having been at work when the survey was conducted, that he worked forty hours that previous week as a "clerk" in a shirt factory, where he earned "1200" dollars during the period beginning twelve months prior to the survey date. The information sheet confirms that Lina DeLillo was proficient in English and communicated these facts and others to the surveyor.[5]

We might reasonably assume that DeLillo's childhood was shaped in profound ways by the experience of being raised in a family of immigrants. The writer Gay Talese, who was also the son of Italian immigrants and also a young boy during World War Two, memorably described the affect and alienation of his own childhood in *Unto the Sons* when he wrote: "I saw myself as an alien, an outsider, a drifter who . . . had arrived by accident. I felt different from my young friends in almost every way, different in the cut of my clothes, the food in my lunchbox, the music I heard at home on the record player, the ideas and inner thoughts I revealed on those rare occasions when I was open and honest. . . . I was olive-skinned in a freckle-faced town."[6]

In its context Talese's description describes his childhood in a town on the New Jersey coast, a place populated by Methodists and Irish immigrants who had been assimilating successfully for a longer time. Talese appears by contrast as a reserved and lonely child, very close to his family yet also sensitive to that which he (and they) were not. It is a common American experience: a child of Arab immigrants might write the same of a Michigan childhood; a son of Koreans might describe it after growing up in Boston; or a daughter of Mexicans might tell the same of her Georgia youth. The drama of the immigrant child is as familiar, difficult, and benign as any American cliché. Would it function to explain the detached, reserved characters who inhabit and narrate DeLillo's novels? Perhaps. If one were to attempt it, however, the more important question might be: at what expense? In using the biography to interpret the fiction, the biography becomes a different sort of fiction—a dishonest one posing as fact. It is at this level of inquiry that DeLillo's novels tend to work, where history becomes difficult and opaque, and only the peculiar reality effect of a novel that deflects biographical interpretation can effectively dramatize its workings.

Conversely, one might recognize in DeLillo's fiction the traits of a person and writer who has made the elemental materials gathered by a first-generation child of immigrants into a rich and powerful source for his art. For instance, DeLillo's fiction often features resourceful women as protagonists who negotiate cultural adversity or who come to points of view that expose some alien quality of a place. Karen in *Mao II* is the perfect example of the latter. As for the former category, critics who accuse DeLillo of being a novelist who writes only about men for an audience of primarily male readers might recall his dramatic characterizations of Babette Gladney (*White Noise*), Brita Nilsson (*Mao II*), Lauren Hartke (*The Body Artist*), and Lianne (*Falling Man*) so as to reconsider that claim's veracity.

After characterization, one might also consider milieu. For example, DeLillo writes often about American mass culture. It contains all those things that the immigrant normally cannot attain but to which the immigrants' children may aspire: baseball, rock and roll, television and radio, fortune. Yet in attaining those things, DeLillo's characters and narrators travel through mass culture in quixotic, often estranged moods. Alienation, loneliness, and anonymity form an existential holy trinity in his prose. DeLillo has often noted modern European authors such as James Joyce or film directors such as Michelangelo Antonioni, artists whose works explore similar emotions, as inspiration for these moods. DeLillo's fiction may be said to translate them to an American idiom and setting. And what if those influences—or one's claiming them—were also a form of assimilation, and of the kind that compensates precisely for the early and difficult feelings that linger from the memory of one's "different" childhood? What if cultural or family influences, considered alone, together, or in combination with others, can help us understand and appreciate the value of a writer's achievement? In this way the traces of DeLillo's status as the son of immigrants might help us understand the relationship between the outsiders who populate his novels but also the role he plays as an artist and observer of American life.

In a 1993 interview, Adam Begley asked DeLillo whether his Italian American roots defined his fiction in some way. DeLillo replied:

> It showed up in early short stories. I think it translates to the novels only in the sense that it gave me a perspective from which to see the larger environment. It's no accident that my first novel was called *Americana*. This was a private declaration of independence, a statement of my intention

> to use the whole picture, the whole culture. America was and is the immigrant's dream, and as the son of two immigrants I was attracted by the sense of possibility that had drawn my parents and grandparents. This was a subject that would allow me to develop a range I hadn't shown in those early stories—a range and a freedom. And I was well into my twenties by this point and had long since left the streets where I'd grown up. Not left them forever—I do want to write about those years. It's just a question of finding the right frame.[7]

"The right frame" would seem to refer to a period in time. It may also invoke a cinema, ekphrastic literature, or paintings that "frame" a subject. We can see here also how DeLillo uses contrast to define the role of autobiography in his fiction: it is something from which to escape, not knowing that you can or will succeed. We might think of it as the immigrant's version of the poet John Keats' concept of negative capability, whereby the poet writes from uncertainty. As the narrator of Bertolt Brecht's "Life Story of the Boxer Samson-Körner" remarks in the opening line of that story, "When they ask you to write something about your own life it isn't all that easy to get it together."[8]

Biographical Criticism

It may come as a surprise that critics are constantly speculating over biographical matters pertinent to DeLillo's writings. Vigorous debate characterizes critical discussions of the relationship between the writer's fiction and what is known of his biography. Some would not concede a relationship at all. There are those, such as Daniel Aaron, who admire DeLillo for avoiding the religious or sociological trappings of ethnic fiction. According to Aaron, those trappings would make DeLillo into a writer incapable of writing about anything more than sectarian matters of identity. "I think it's worth noting," Aaron wrote, "that nothing in his novels suggests a suppressed 'Italian foundation'; hardly a vibration betrays an ethnic consciousness."[9] Without diminishing the role of the writer's ethnicity, Frank Lentricchia makes the case for DeLillo's "American" (as opposed to ethno-provincial) ambitions.[10]

By contrast, there are critics who persuasively argue that DeLillo's prose explicitly alludes to his ethnic, urban milieu, and that his Italian American biography underscores a powerful sense of ethnicity in his writings (even if it may not provide direct sources for that sense). In his landmark study *Italian Signs, American Streets* (1996), Fred Gardaphé persuasively counters Aaron's argument that DeLillo's fiction avoids the trappings of an ethnic writer. Gardaphé instead notes that DeLillo's Italian American family history and the ethnic, urban milieu of his youth converge in a "masquerade" that confirms his fiction's roots in American ethnic experience.[11] Addressing perhaps Aaron's refusal to admit the import of Catholicism in DeLillo's fiction, Amy Hungerford has recently argued that DeLillo's prose is structured upon a profound sense of Catholic ritual.[12] Working from the ritual narrative structures in DeLillo's fiction, Hungerford describes how DeLillo's novels refract secular and religious shifts in late-twentieth-century American culture. It is interesting to note that while DeLillo's readers are divided in rather complicated ways concerning his Catholicism, critics of Catholic-American literature do not include Don DeLillo (or Toni Morrison) in the interesting minor field of literary criticism devoted to Catholic writers who write or have written in the United States.[13]

Whereas Gardaphé refers to sociological and linguistic frameworks of ethnicity in his critical reading of DeLillo and Hungerford refers to theology in her work, other critics have written about DeLillo's rendering of ethnicity in a way other than in a specific form (that is, "Italian"). Critic Biman Basu has paired the general problematic of ethnicity with the role of technology in DeLillo's fiction. Technology plays important roles in DeLillo's fiction, and it is, together with ethnicity, also one of the more popular critical categories used to discuss his work (though it is not as divisive as the latter category). In his article Basu reviews how DeLillo's *White Noise* offers a subtle parody of the Taylor-Fordist model of industrial labor management in which immigrants are coded as prosthetic extensions of industrial machinery.[14] Basu does not narrow the field to any particular ethnicity but insightfully (and correctly) regards the category in more general terms so as to appreciate how *White Noise* distinguishes what we might describe as ethnic European, blue-collar labor from the Caucasian professional class of Anglo-Saxon descent in American society.

Other critics have been more forceful in claiming the relationships between DeLillo's ethnicity and his fiction, and with some success. I have noted the examples of Basu, Hungerford, and Gardaphé, however, because they are careful to avoid reducing DeLillo's fiction to an ethnic or ethno-religious identity. The fact that critics generally admit this caveat confirms the hazards of using DeLillo's biography as a key to interpreting his fiction. Yet the traces of ethnic language identified by Gardaphé, the ethno-religious features revealed by Hungerford, or the broader problematic of "techno-ethnicity" discussed by Basu suggest that despite DeLillo's ambitions to be considered an "American" (as opposed to Italian American) writer, his life, family history, and experience as the child of immigrants coexist with what Lentricchia and Aaron call the "American" ambitions of his novels. One might say the two are inseparable. For instance, DeLillo has a remarkable ear for ethnic dialects, and not only Italian American habits of speech; the nuns who speak in a German American dialect in the penultimate chapter of *White Noise* (1985) exemplify the point. In this sense DeLillo's "ethnicity" appears as a cosmopolitan awareness of the different ethnic groups who in their sum made up the American population during the twentieth century. More broadly, ethnicity (whether specific or cosmopolitan) indicates a social process of assimilation typical across American history. It is a process subject to postmodern rendering in that it often takes form as a yearning for a lost identity that is manifest, counterintuitively, as an escape from it. In certain moments in DeLillo's fiction (one thinks of the Jewish football player Anatole Bloomberg in his 1973 novel *End Zone*), it appears as a parody of that very process. Who is to say the ethnic experience is not all these things, and more, in DeLillo's America?

In sum, biographical criticism of DeLillo's writings constitutes a consistent, insightful line of thinking about his fiction. The line is more difficult and developed than it may at first appear, and more compelling than readers who resist such arguments would have one believe. DeLillo's biography does indeed suggest settings, languages, histories, figures, and moods that are unlike those found in his fiction. We may think of them as disconnected, even antagonistic, but perhaps it is in recognizing the murmurs of the largely inaccessible conversation between them that we begin to hear the America of DeLillo's later fiction after all. Without the mystery and mise-en-scène of his biography, it would be more difficult to appreciate the montage of his literary career.

Given the suggestive inconsistencies of the official record, we can assign the DeLillo family history and the writer's childhood to experiences that typify European, and specifically Italian, immigration and assimilation to the United States during the early twentieth century. It is not a narrative lost to history but one that belongs to its silent crowd. The occasional critic has bid it speak. The crowd does not always oblige.

Don DeLillo's family returned to New York City at some point following its Pennsylvania sojourn. There he lived in the borough of the Bronx, in the Italian American neighborhood that lines Arthur Avenue. It is today, as it was then, both a neighborhood and a world. As was typical of many historic ethnic communities in the United States, many of its youth eventually left and moved out of the city, settling in the growing suburbs and the provinces of mass culture.

DeLillo belongs to a generation of major American writers who were born during the Great Depression. As such they came of age during the novel's alleged high-water mark in American history and successfully carried its tradition to the future. In DeLillo's case the past is often a densely populated space, one from which to flee (often to the sparse landscapes of the American

Southwest). Whether in centrifugal flight from them or centripetal fall into them, DeLillo's fiction is particularly attuned to "crowds," a major theme of his work. DeLillo does not belong to the generation born after World War II, the so-called baby boomers. Yet because he was raised primarily in New York City, a cultural capital that hosts the art, wealth, excitement, and generations of that population explosion, it is no wonder that DeLillo developed an early and consistent interest in describing the moods and movements of great masses of people. (One also finds different versions of migrations in the writers named above.) DeLillo has commented at times on the cultural influences offered to him by New York City during the 1950s. He counts among them the jazz music scene of Greenwich Village, institutions such as the Museum of Modern Art, and the city's postwar sports culture, particularly that of its three baseball teams (the Giants, Dodgers, and Yankees).[15]

As noted earlier, DeLillo's career begins at the tail end of the novel's cultural dominance but also at the moment when its broadest readership was concentrated in (and also beginning to leave) urban spaces that defined American life and culture at the height of its global influence. Perched at a vantage slightly ahead of that later crowd, DeLillo's career self-consciously enters the tradition of American literary fiction at precisely that point—1960—when critics mark its initial decline. In retrospect, as one looks over a half century of his work, his fiction as a whole offers something of an allegory of that generational movement (a point that I believe resonates with baby boomers, who are his primary audience).

As he uses the novel to narrate the moods and movements of that crowd, DeLillo innovates the novel's subjects, characters, narration, language, and dialogue. Are his innovations a form of nostalgia for a dying art? Like the crowd, nostalgia is a frequent subject in DeLillo's novels, but nostalgia never appears in his work as naïve sentiment. DeLillo's fiction instead offers history as comedy and terror, anxiety and wonder, visions and words. If there is nostalgia, the reader is generally made to feel that nostalgia performs some other work by asking us to consider how we experience history, language, and life in aesthetic forms. Why retreat into sentimental convention and cliché, his fiction seems to ask, when the novel can offer so much more?

After the novel and the crowd, there is the market. It is the common ground of exchange on which they meet. With more than a half century of fiction to his credit, DeLillo's career currently finds itself in the midst of one of the more interesting periods in the history of the novel, when digital technologies tempt literary writers to find new modes of expression. DeLillo composes his novels in an age when, for the first time in human history, we do not only print them on paper, but write (and read) them in light. Suspended as the novel is between debates over "old" print and broadcast media on the one hand and the "new" digital media on the other, this transitional moment would seem the perfect match for one of DeLillo's favorite moods. I refer here to those scenes in which he balances characters between solitude and something that has not yet occurred or begun to register in a character, narrator, or reader's mind: in *Libra* one man enters a Dallas building and waits with a rifle, while in *Falling Man* another man exits bleeding from a New York City skyscraper during a terrorist attack; in *Mao II* a woman photographs a glowing Lebanese battlefield at night, while in *The Body Artist* another prepares her body for imminent performance in a (seemingly) empty house on the New England coast. Here we find the antithesis to "the crowd"—a profoundly individual sense of being outside yet somehow within the moment, as artists work with care at its fraying edges and characters watch murderers try to disrupt it with their violence. Implicitly and explicitly, this mood slows literary narration down to a pace that resembles slow motion (as in the final lines of his 1985 novel *White Noise*). In doing so, DeLillo makes a case for the novel's capacity to articulate philosophical questions about how readers experience time and thereby affirm the philosophical as well as aesthetic import of the novel, while also preventing it from being reduced to an easy commodity. One might say DeLillo's fiction performs a high-wire act that moves between individuals and crowds; one might also say there are only individuals on the wire, and the crowded marketplace waits to catch them when they fall.

In these ways and others, post–World War II America has a special status in DeLillo's fiction. Indeed, his novels rarely venture into historical territory prior to World War II. (Those parts of *Libra* devoted to Lee Harvey Oswald's childhood are the exception.) The Cold War, the *Pax Americana,* and the economic "boom" of postwar mass culture are DeLillo's home turf; and he devotes substantial parts or entire novels to its cities, small towns, and suburbs. Sprawling cities, and New York in particular, appear in other works where the riptides of mass culture, driven by media and money, carry characters through neon-lit and liquid-crystal aggregations of recent historical time. This is particularly true of the historical novel *Underworld* (1997) as well as the more contemporary novels *Mao II* (1991) and *Cosmopolis* (2003).

Two figures appear exceptional in the late-twentieth-century milieu of DeLillo's fiction. They are the tyrant and the crowd. If we were to consider that era in terms of a great chain of being, wherein certain life forms are arranged into hierarchies, we would find the political tyrant at the top of the chain and the crowd near the bottom. Dictators, tyrants, and prophets often haunt DeLillo's fiction. They include secular political figures such as Chairman Mao (*Mao II*), Colonel Qaddafi (*White Noise*), and Adolf Hitler (*Running Dog,*

White Noise), religious figures such as the Ayatollah Khomeini (*Mao II*), and terrorists with theologically rooted political aspirations such as "Bill Lawton" (a child's name for [Usama] bin Laden in *Falling Man*). Their desire to shape history and to control people takes suicidal form for their subjects and genocidal form for their enemies. A disturbing man in DeLillo's short story "Baader-Meinhof" makes the point in this way when he interrupts a woman contemplating paintings of dead terrorists: "When they're not killing other people, they are killing themselves."[16] In another recent short story entitled "Hammer and Sickle," DeLillo's narrator (an imprisoned investor) notes that the names of Communist leaders being recited in a faux newscast by his daughters "were immense footprints on history."[17] The latter, mythic proportion may be said to facilitate the former murderous effect. DeLillo's fiction often depicts the two along interwoven trajectories: how characters perceive terrorists as well as the way in which the mass media magnify terrorists (and also shape characters' perceptions). In the first short story quoted above, for example, the discussion turns to whether the German authorities killed the terrorists in their jail cells and whether the paintings imply or refuse such interpretations. In DeLillo's fiction art has the unique capacity to complicate the way we regard such figures, resisting any reductive interpretation. Unlike the mass media, fiction functions as antimedia in such moments.

DeLillo has written on murderous tyrants and their acolytes in modes other than fiction, composing essays on the topic at certain times. One would not suggest that DeLillo is a public intellectual in the manner of a professor or politician but rather that his forays into the essay (it is a literary form, after all) transpose his art (though never entirely) into the more discursive forums and debates of the public sphere. As in his fiction, the historical fascination with tyrants and terrorists is a recurrent theme in the few essays he has published. I use the word "fascination" here to invoke Susan Sontag's famous essay, first published in 1975, on the German filmmaker Leni Riefenstahl, entitled "Fascinating Fascism." Sontag's essay argued that the staging of fascist politics involves carefully choreographed displays of control; through the media, those assemblies subjugate audiences to the will of another entity (the state, embodied by a dictator). Sontag noted that the audience derives a certain masochistic pleasure from the experience of being rendered powerless. In this way she criticized audiences and intellectuals who contributed to the "de-Nazification" of Riefenstahl's films and also the revival of interest in early- to mid-twentieth-century fascist aesthetics (especially in cinema) that was taking place in the 1970s.

DeLillo also regarded the cultural dynamics of fascism in a rare critical essay entitled "Silhouette City: Hitler, Manson and the Millennium" (1989).

In that essay he extended elements of Sontag's argument in another direction: to the future. Using Norman Cohn's 1957 *Pursuit of the Millennium: Revolutionary Messianism in Medieval and Reformation Europe and Its Bearing on Modern Totalitarian Movements,* DeLillo reviews a shift in American culture: he claims that assassins, crazed with apocalyptic fantasies, share a territory with cults (such as the Manson Family) and extremist groups (primarily neo-Nazis) who endorse similar eschatological beliefs. DeLillo writes: "The barricaded gunman is a lyrical fixture of our time. He is what remains of the wilderness and he feels a pulse in his brain that beats for desolation. Bring it all down" (350). DeLillo elaborates here the "mountain" characters of Riefenstahl's cinema in this passage, but he adds a new twist: they do not represent effective, popular political movements sprung from an individual or folk imaginary. Rather, they populate the media, which in turn use them to colonize the imagination of viewers with apocalyptic visual allegories of mass death, economic disaster, industrial accident, natural catastrophe, and, perhaps most distressing of all, a world without information or electronic media.

The figures that DeLillo described in "Silhouette City: Hitler, Manson and the Millennium" had already a prominent place in his fiction (and the millennium would appear to be an important end, and also new beginning, in his later fiction). We find those characters in the utopian splinter group that seeks the mysterious "product" in *Great Jones Street* (1973), the collectors who seek the lost film shot in Hitler's bunker in *Running Dog* (1978), and the convicted gunman who corresponds with Jack Gladney's son Heinrich in *White Noise* (1985); indeed, the compelling *Libra,* a novel about the assassin Lee Harvey Oswald, would seem to exploit that very same fascination, yet to some less salacious and more thoughtful end. (DeLillo never entirely judges these fringe characters and seems more interested in their media effect, satiric potential, or their actual biographies, thereby avoiding Sontag's moralisms.) DeLillo's breakthrough novel *White Noise* is itself an extended rumination on some of the questions raised by Sontag and recast by DeLillo into a media-fueled frenzy of chemical disasters (both pharmaceutical and environmental). Who can read the passages in that novel describing Jack Gladney's attempts to speak the German language and not think of Riefenstahl's deliberate close-up shots of Hitler's or Himmler's bizarre and contorted elocutions in *Triumph of the Will*?[18] Like artists, these apocalyptic figures shape the way we perceive, think about, and experience the world; unlike artists, no good ever comes from their ambitions to divert the will of the masses away from history. Try as murderers and tyrants might to control and deform a people, they never conquer it. "The future," DeLillo writes in *Mao II,* "belongs to crowds." One might read the sentence as the admission of the individual's historical defeat. In another sense, it suggests the amorphous intelligence of populations who will sooner or later figure out that some prophetic criminal deceives them.

There is a third and all-important figure that occupies the lowest and most vulnerable point of this hierarchy. It is the individual imagination. Imagination communicates the moral authority of art, the power of wit, and the capacity for love. It navigates trauma and grief. Ambiguous at times, it can also display a quality that critics sometimes refer to as the "paranoid" element of postmodern fiction. The term is sometimes mistakenly used to attribute falsehood and a frivolous sense of history to DeLillo and other writers. When individual characters seek out alternate explanations for events in their lives, they behave like crazy biographers reorganizing the facts and phenomena of their lives into new arrangements. Fancy then gets the best of them. In the worst cases they become enchanted by a brutal ideology or a cult. In the best cases they attain an understanding of their relationship to the world that might be described as clear, calm, or confident. (The character Lianne in the 2007 novel *Falling Man* exemplifies all three states.) What begins with crowds and tyrants often ends in DeLillo's fiction with serene detachment, a movement often represented in geographic terms. For example, his characters often travel from the crowded American Northeast to the open spaces of the American Southwest, where they look for solace in the latter's ascetic spaces. They do not always find it there. We see this when Keith Neudecker, Lianne's estranged husband, dissolves into the Nevada casinos in the aforementioned *Falling Man*, in what seems a failed attempt to escape the memory of the terrorist attack that destroyed his office building and killed his friends and colleagues on September 11, 2001. By contrast, Lianne remains in the city, her life, memory, and imagination invincible.

Artists appear with regularity as fictional characters in his novels, and DeLillo affords to them a unique if somewhat turbulent status. The novelist Bill Gray in *Mao II* (1991) is the most widely discussed of the lot. Bill Gray stands in that book as a figure for the institution of the modern novel. It is a figure under siege by theological orthodoxy, ideological fanaticism, and their terrorist acolytes. According to Bill Gray, the novel and novelist are not in decline: they and the freedom of expression they represent are diminished by proportion to the physical violence and media spectacle of contemporary terrorism. "What terrorists gain, novelists lose" (157), says Bill while meeting with George, an intellectual and spokesperson for the Lebanese Maoist terrorists who have kidnapped a young and completely unknown Swiss poet. Bill is trying to arrange a prisoner swap in which he would become a hostage in exchange for the young poet's freedom. The reader unfamiliar with DeLillo's writings should not expect a simple or sentimental resolution of Bill Gray's situation; such is always the case in DeLillo's fiction. DeLillo often depicts novelists and other artists as characters negotiating public scrutiny, commercial pressure, or ethical questions to conserve a private space for individual creativity (or, in Bill Gray's case, to selflessly abandon that privacy in the interest of protecting the rights of another writer). Readers have devoted increased attention to this aspect of DeLillo's career in recent years. For example, DeLillo scholar Mark Osteen has perceptively noted that these characters exist in a contradiction wherein they "must both engage their society and maintain a critical distance from its blinding glare and deafening buzz."[19]

In his depictions of crowds, tyrants, and artists, DeLillo would seem a representative of a specific generation who watched post–World War II America develop (and its population move) into new forms and habits during that era. One must include technology among those forms. As noted in the preface and earlier in the present chapter, American writers have always written with American media in mind. Just as Hawthorne eventually contended with the railroad and the daguerreotype in *The House of the Seven Gables* (1851), later American writers had to contend with new technologies and emergent communications media in particular. DeLillo's American education in the 1950s and his early career as a writer coincided after all with a remarkable era of economic prosperity, a prosperity that entirely transformed American mass media culture. Inexpensive paperbacks began to displace hardbound books, glossy color magazines competed with black-and-white newspapers, and television replaced radio as the most popular form of broadcasting. Older media forms such as cinema won a new cultural prestige as art forms. All of these were integrated into new transportation systems: air travel, for instance, allowed a traveler to access all these media in an airport that was also a hub of transit for information as well as people. In addition, new computing technologies—IBM punch-card machines, Apple personal computers, the World Wide Web, the touchscreen smart phone—appeared with increasing frequency. DeLillo's later writings, and particularly the novel *Cosmopolis* (2003), depict the so-called New Media, but his 1998 play *Valparaiso* offers perhaps the most comprehensive view, as it connects the mid-century geographic disorientation of air travel with late-twentieth-century media technologies.

Over the course of more than a half century of writing, Don DeLillo's fiction has communicated how characters, readers, and art experience media both old and new, doing so in ways that many consider to be unique in the history of American literary writing. DeLillo works through the implications of those technologies. As noted above, DeLillo was old enough during the 1950s to observe these early changes and later to capture them in his art.

Perhaps this is the historical vantage afforded to those who remember times in which such things did not yet exist, but who also have the sensibility never to accept change at face value.

DeLillo gathers all these interests into his novels. He notes that he first began thinking of writing while he was a student in high school (1950–1954) and that his first inspirations included the great modern authors such as Faulkner, Joyce, Hemingway, and others.[20] American mass culture was in ascent at that time, complicating the notions of modernity held by a prior generation of writers. The old lines between high culture and mass low culture become unclear as forms mingled in new and astounding ways. In the second half of the twentieth century, we find artists mixing media, challenging notions of cultural superiority as they repossessed and reinvented older artistic forms and other media. In literary fiction, writers incorporate the radio (see Norman Mailer, Ishmael Reed), combine journalism with literary narrative (Truman Capote, Joan Didion), mix comic strips with the literary novel (Jay Cantor, Art Spiegelman), and revise and integrate historical materials into their fiction (Toni Morrison, Philip Roth, E. L. Doctorow). Literary tradition also becomes a source for the recycling of older materials: Kathy Acker revises Charles Dickens, Joyce Carol Oates rewrites Henry James, and so on. (One might say there are also analogous impulses in literary criticism of the era.) In his own career, DeLillo used elements of the sports novel (*End Zone*), the spy thriller (*Running Dog*), and the biography (*Libra*), and also appropriated nongeneric modes of writing, such as the novel of psychological realism (*The Body Artist*), for his fiction. He has used government documents as source materials (*The Warren Report* was a source for *Libra*), and his novels sometimes integrate visual materials into their layout and design (the press release in *Great Jones Street,* the newspaper front page in *Pafko at the Wall,* news photographs in *Mao II*).

After literature, cinema is the most important source of narrative technique, as well as affect, in DeLillo's fiction. Like the novel, it is a popular art form, but also one whose ambitions and achievements were recognized as prestigious, "important," during the great wave of foreign films and "great directors" (the so-called auteurs) who gained unprecedented success in the United States after World War II. Watching cinema—an obvious influence on his work, and one he proclaims as formative—DeLillo adopted to his fiction cinematic techniques used by modern directors. (He has named Antonioni, Kubrick, Godard, Fellini, Bergman, and Hawks as being among his favorite directors.)[21]

In his use of cinema, we find the visual analog to the democratic impulse that shapes DeLillo's aesthetic. He will at times combine literary language with visual-cinematic narrative technique in his fiction, and to spectacular effect. Consider the opening scene of his novel *Underworld* (1997), when the teenager Cotter Martin waits for his chance to jump the turnstiles and enter the Polo Grounds to watch a baseball game. He is watching and also "part of an assembling crowd" (11). He makes his move, avoids the rush of security guards, and enters the stadium. The game begins. The narration pans across the grandstands like a motion picture camera. We see a close-up shot of "Frank Sinatra, Jackie Gleason and Toots Shor" (17), the titans of music, television and nightclub entertainment, sitting near FBI Director J. Edgar Hoover. Banter. The perspective cuts to the outfield and back to young Cotter watching the game. The setting is popular, the staging cinematic; the boy is wide-eyed and happy. We might recall when the narrator of Albert Camus's novel *The Fall* (1956) says, "Even now, the Sunday matches in an overflowing stadium, and the theater, which I loved with great passion, are the only places in the world where I feel innocent."[22] As Cotter enjoys the game, a man named Rafferty—Special Agent Rafferty—kneels beside Director Hoover. Hoover leaves his seat and the two men ascend the stairs, where Rafferty informs the director that "the Soviet Union has conducted an atomic test at a secret location" (23). When the narrative returns to Cotter a few pages later, a man named Bill tells him that, in baseball, "You do what they did before you" (31). The reader, who is privy to information to which Cotter is not, senses a change in the mood, a break with the past. Something unprecedented has happened on the other side of the world, and something more is about to happen in the game. The innocence of Camus's narrator is shattered by the panoramic scope of DeLillo's narration. The reader enters history. Lines we assume to divide observer from participant, or character from reader—a sort of literary fourth wall—are erased. We might say that whereas Camus's narrator plays a solo, DeLillo, in his narration, conducts a symphony, and it is the crowd that plays the instruments.

An ethnic and primarily urban childhood during the Great Depression and the Second World War, followed by teenage life in high school (Cardinal Hayes High School in the Bronx) and college (Fordham, also in the Bronx) during the Eisenhower decade: these are the prelude to Don DeLillo's career. Following the symphonic motif (or, if you prefer, the four-part suite of Coltrane's *A Love Supreme*), this book divides DeLillo's writing career into four periods. The first is that from 1960 to 1971, during which he published only short stories. The second is from 1971 to 1985, during which he published his first seven novels, his first essays, and his first play. The third is from 1985 to 1997, the period of his greatest popularity, during which four novels were published, as well as a second play. (This is also the period of his involvement in the "Rushdie Affair" and his first explicit advocacy of free speech.) Finally, there is the period from 2000 to the present time, during which he published four short novels, wrote a screenplay that was made into a feature film, published numerous new stories, a third play, and several essays.

The frequency of DeLillo's early publications should not obscure a very important point about his career. While DeLillo composed seven novels during the second period of his career (1971–85), he only reached a broad readership, and its attendant commercial success and critical acclaim, with the publication of *White Noise* in 1985. From 1960 to 1985, he worked in relative anonymity, devoted "like a donut-maker, only slower" to the craft of writing: a quarter century, 25 years, 300 months, 9,125 days (give or take a few, depending on where the leap years fall), 21,900 hours, 1,314,000 minutes, nearly 80 billion seconds. Here is a possible source for another feature of DeLillo's writing: his interest in writing about human time and memory as if it moved at a glacial pace. His own career developed, after all, with a geological patience. One can assume that Don DeLillo was always a renowned and recognizable writer. To do so, however, is to ignore the fact that the first half of his career was relatively unheralded. DeLillo's evaluation of those early stories and novels is that they were "undeveloped."[23] If we take his view to be a credible one—and the work is admittedly uneven in quality—it also affirms the intelligence of his readership: greater numbers of readers embraced his books when DeLillo's fiction achieved the style for which he is now praised.

Conversely, the precedent can also tarnish the later achievement. It is easy to look back at DeLillo's early writings and recognize elements that would become more pronounced in the later, more famous, or "developed," works. Fate, it would seem. Yet DeLillo's novels published between 1985 and 1997 mark a run matched by few American writers. DeLillo succeeded in reaching an extraordinarily large international audience and sustaining it. His readership in the United States was equally broad and diverse. Critical acclaim and commercial success followed, and his writings won nearly every national and international literary award. Fate is rarely so generous; one might again consider the role that twenty-five years of solitary labor played in this later success.

The period in question spans four novels. Beginning with *White Noise* (1985), it includes *Libra* (1988), *Mao II* (1991), and *Underworld* (1997). Frank Lentricchia offers a useful summary of the awards DeLillo received during the 1980s, but it is necessary to extend the list to include the later books.[24] During the dozen years that constitute the period in question, DeLillo won the National Book Award for *White Noise* and the Pen/Faulkner Award for *Mao II*. Had he won the Pulitzer Prize for fiction (both *Mao II* and *Underworld* were finalists), he would have gained the triple crown of American literary awards. Internationally, his writings of that period won the *Irish Times* Aer Lingus Prize for International Fiction, the Jerusalem Prize, and the Bachelli Prize for International Fiction. In 1995 he won the Lilla Wallace Reader's Digest Award for his work among patients of Alzheimer's disease (an experience that may have provided source material for the character Lianne Glenn in his 2007 novel *Falling Man*).[25] The run concluded with the prestigious William Dean Howells Medal for *Underworld*. Readers may think that the prizes are no guarantee of literary merit. This is true. But one must also remember that most of the prizes are judged and awarded by fellow writers, and no single prize ever features the same jury. Plus, the prizes DeLillo earned involve not only awards for literary merit but for ancillary activities, including service to his community and advocacy on behalf of free speech.

In addition to earning the recognition of his peers, the period 1985–97 constitutes a remarkable period in the printing and sale of DeLillo's works. A cynic might say the prizes he won are merely the effect of this surge in printed copies. This may also be true. It does not, however, dismiss the quality of books that were printed, or reprinted, or that DeLillo—who had been until that time a rather obscure writer of postmodern genre fiction—had popularized postmodern fiction on an unprecedented scale. *Americana,* DeLillo's first novel, had a first printing of 4,500 copies. *White Noise* had a first printing of 25,000, and *Libra* 75,000. Various sources note that the first printing of *Underworld* was 450,000 copies. Beginning in the mid-1980s after the success of *White Noise,* Penguin Books reissued DeLillo's first three novels (*Americana, End Zone,* and *Great Jones Street*) in new paperback editions; these were followed, beginning in 1989, by new Vintage paperback editions of *Ratner's Star, Players, Running Dog,* and *The Names* (the four novels immediately prior to *White Noise*). It is reasonable to estimate that by the mid-1990s the number of copies of DeLillo's novels made available to readers numbered in the millions.

Capable reviewers and critics discovered DeLillo's fiction during this time and fueled the rush of interest. (Again, one can take the cynical view.) They emerged from a critical readership that first formed during the 1970s. In a very useful survey of the early criticism of DeLillo's work, Hugh Ruppersburg and Tim Engles divide that early readership into distinct parts: "The first begins with *Americana* in 1971 and extends through *The Names* in 1982. During this phase reviewers began to recognize DeLillo's abilities as a novelist, his interest in 'ideas,' and skill with language and humor."[26] Prominent reviewers included novelists such as Joyce Carol Oates, Anthony Burgess, and John Updike (not all of whom were kind in assessing DeLillo's novels). A second group emerges during the mid- to late 1980s as scholars such as Tom LeClair,

Frank Lentricchia, David Cowart, John McClure, and others published books, edited collections of essays, and wrote articles and book chapters devoted to DeLillo's writings. (LeClair was also one of DeLillo's first interviewers, in 1982.) Special issues of major scholarly journals collected articles devoted to DeLillo's writings, conferences were held to discuss his work, and a Don DeLillo Society was formed. Online forums, reader's guides, and websites devoted to DeLillo began to appear during the 1990s. Journalists and fellow writers continue to write about and explain DeLillo to the new audiences that gather to read his works, and by the 2000s these varied readerships came to constitute a diverse and compelling international readership. DeLillo has warmly acknowledged its representatives in industry and culture on occasion by commemorating an editor (Nan Graham, December 2012) or a fellow writer (David Foster Wallace, October 2008). At a symposium in April 2013, he read an excerpt from *Underworld* at Duke University on the occasion of Frank Lentricchia's retirement.

I do not present the scale of DeLillo's acclaim and success to justify the literary merits of his novels. Rather, I would like to think that we continue to live in a culture capable of recognizing and rewarding a writer's imagination and achievement. Literary writers rarely achieve such status; yet when they do it would seem necessary to consider that status in honest terms. This, I believe, is also the role of criticism. Nonetheless, I would also caution that regarding DeLillo's astonishing accomplishments and success of the period 1985–97 one can also become distracted by their "aura," to invoke Murray Siskind's famous discussion of "THE MOST PHOTOGRAPHED BARN IN AMERICA" from the novel *White Noise.* Perhaps the scale of DeLillo's success has made difficult to appreciate dispassionately the four novels of this period. We see their glory and praise, but not their words. This problem reminds us that the scale of that success does not confirm the value of the novels in question. Rather, the novels belittle that success—"economize it"—so that readers might adjust their focus and perspective to the printed page. Can one admit success without precluding literary accomplishment? Is the fiction a key to the biography or vice versa? Do we see the barn or only the photo of the barn? Can a reader enjoy *White Noise* without considering everything that has been written on it? Or must we read in light of such histories, negotiating their habits and conflicts? If so, what autonomy remains for us, as readers, to decide how to read, enjoy, or discuss a novel? If we take the negative view, we appear in the grim "dead end" situation of the character of Gary Harkness in DeLillo's early novel *End Zone,* trapped by languages and forces we cannot control or comprehend. If we take the optimistic view, which is more common yet also more delicate in DeLillo's later fiction, we affirm that it is only by entering into dialogue with history, art, and language art that we may ultimately become free.

A forgotten photograph, lost in the data deluge of American print, serves to bring this preliminary discussion to an appropriate conclusion. On September 16, 1997, DeLillo became the first writer to have his photograph printed in color in the *New York Times*. "The Grey Lady" had always preferred the documentary sobriety of black-and-white images, but had finally relented to new technologies for newspaper print, technologies that made the color printing process less difficult and costly. There were also competitors who had already made the change, and were gaining ground, to consider. In addition to technology and market share, there was a third factor: advertising. Long the pillar of revenue in print journalism, advertising was also a highly aestheticized visual form of commercial capitalism. Who better than Don DeLillo, a writer who had written a great deal about American advertising and consumer culture, to stand before the window of a small business in his old Bronx neighborhood and have his photo taken to represent the paradox and anachronism of the moment? DeLillo, who has written consistently and beautifully about business and advertising, seemed a perfect choice for this combination of the mundane and the extraordinary. After all, his fiction had turned the flow of that data back upon itself in ways that make us aware of its bidirectional flow, as if to remind us that as it speaks to us, we also speak to it. This too is the role of the novel and the novelist.

Unbeknownst to readers holding that newspaper in 1997, the American publishing industry would be a much different place in less than a decade's time. DeLillo's America had long been a wonderland of radio signals, print advertisement, television commercials, movie theaters, and pop songs, with an occasional computer screen. They were the machines of the messengers. Today, they are all absorbed and absorbing the digital revolution that was then in its infancy. The color photograph (reproduced in black and white on the cover of this book), ironically showing DeLillo at his old haunts, appeared at a threshold: writing and writers would never be the same. We see it creeping into his fiction already with his next novel, *The Body Artist*, in which the protagonist Lauren Hartke sits at her computer screen for hours, transfixed by a camera that broadcasts a dark Finnish highway over the Internet, cars traveling on the road. She is hypnotized by this new thing. She wonders what to make of it.

At the same time, even as it communicates wonder before the violence and comedy of contemporary life, DeLillo's fiction also prepared us for what art and artists would become in a new and rapidly emerging world. It described its pleasure as well as suspicion, and it combined nostalgia with regret. His fiction always depicted America moving from the industrial age into the age of data and information, images and simulation. By the 1990s, when the Cold War ended and the Internet made its public debut, DeLillo was in a position to make art and sense of it all. This was not his paranoia, or prophecy, or hindsight, or good fortune. It was instead a matter of simply paying attention, and using both his practiced techniques and those others shared among modern artists, so as to describe the change with imagination. There is in this sense little mystery, and only hard work, to credit for his achievement. But even then, when looking upon that color photograph printed near to the close of the twentieth century, we are reminded of how and when the old world of print pages, binding, and ink began its confused migration to bits of data and pulses of light. Two worlds, one more permanent and tangible, the other ephemeral and numinous, converge on that threshold. Through the camera lens does the writer stare into our world, or do we spy into his?

CHAPTER 2

Jargon and Genre

Americana, End Zone, and *Great Jones Street*

Imagine a customer browsing an independent bookstore's shelves in 1971. It is mid-June, and this avid book buyer is looking for summer reading. Established authors—Walker Percy, Leon Uris, Mary McCarthy—have new fiction on the best-seller lists (a young critic named Helen Vendler has recently sung the praises of McCarthy's latest novel), and Sylvia Plath's posthumous sensation *The Bell Jar* comes highly recommended, too. The bookstore is small, with a limited stock of recent titles, and the only advertising consists of clipped reviews tacked to a cork board. The customer sometimes relies on the owners, who know their patrons' tastes, to recommend books. At this time, however, one of the owners is busy with another customer, and the other has crossed the street to purchase a roll of receipt paper from the stationer. The customer browses restlessly, in the mood for something unheralded and new.

One book catches the browser's eye. It is entitled *Americana,* and its author's name is Don DeLillo. The spine reveals its publisher as the prestigious Houghton Mifflin Company of Boston. The back cover of the dust jacket features a large black-and-white portrait of the author shot in natural light. It shows a pensive man looking down and away. The photo's chiaroscuro suggests staging and purpose. A biographical note on the inside back flap is similarly understated. It reads: "Don DeLillo was born and lives in New York City. *Americana* is his first novel." Here are a reputable publisher, biographical minimalism, an artful photograph, and perhaps a hint of mystery.[1]

The front of the dust jacket is white and largely blank. A single horizontal strip containing a collage of images wraps across the cover from the book's spine. The collage sequence in that strip shows, from left to right, a face (its nose and left eye) behind a camera of some sort (the eye peering through the lens), a viewfinder, a hand against the viewfinder, and a second left eye that is nearly identical to the first (but this time not encircled by a lens). A landscape is reflected in the viewfinder's lens. The front cover communicates that the novel has something to do with photography, perception, and landscapes. Perhaps Walker Percy's *The Moviegoer* (1961) comes to mind. In its tasteful yet somewhat esoteric design, the publisher is deliberately saying something about the novel's story but also presenting the book itself as a sort of artistic commodity.

Decades later the reader may recall this as a frequent pattern in the design of DeLillo's books. (This is not to suggest he has some hand in the design, only that his publishers apparently take care to read the novels and think the matter through.) For now, the reader takes a chance and purchases the novel, finding upon reading it that the dust jacket of *Americana* indicates several key features of DeLillo's early fiction. In the first place, it is averse to autobiography. In the second, DeLillo's settings, like the dust jacket, suggest an interest in how we perceive objects and also with landscapes that feature empty or negative space (a theme that never vanishes from DeLillo's fiction). Third, as a form of advertising, the dust jacket avoids easy commercialism (although such dust jackets have always appealed to the tastes of certain consumers). Indeed, advertising will play unusual roles in his fiction, roles that are often comic, yet sometimes unnerving.

This is all apparent in retrospect, of course, and indicates that from the start of his career DeLillo had ambitions to modify how readers experience literature. By mixing media (cinema and modern literature in *Americana,* still life painting and a novel about grief in *Falling Man,* pop music lyrics and the detective novel in *Great Jones Street,* and so on), DeLillo's novels ask readers to consider familiar objects and emotions in new ways. The novels ask: how do we draw pleasure from novels? What relations might novels have with other art forms in this day and age? How do we consume art, and are we limited to a certain range of options for the experience of it? Can we find new ways to write literary fiction that will alter our perception of art and life? Drawing these questions to the surface, DeLillo embodies them in the roles that artists play in his novels. Writers, sculptors, performance artist, filmmakers, and poets often appear in them. Whether we consider them in terms of commodities or characters, the point of DeLillo's books lies here: they ask readers to consider, take pleasure from, and defend the value of literary expression. Hence we should note that, beginning with its cover design and coursing through the pages of that first novel, DeLillo was elaborating these questions from the beginning of his career. Even at that time, in an age of "mass media" and print culture, his novels aspired to connect with readers at the intersection where commodities and how we consume them mingle with our dread and our delight. The dust jacket of the first edition of DeLillo's first novel already communicates this ambition in some form, and it is an ambition that will take remarkable forms of urgency and prescience in his later novels.

The problem with assessing a first novel is that we always read it in light of its writer's later works (assuming that such works exist). If it is well written, a first published novel may project the illusion of mastery, or what we metaphorically describe as a "maturity of style." The narration may seem pitch-perfect, the dialogue may strike all the right notes, and the words sound harmonious, arranged in delightful, unexpected ways as they assemble in the form of a plot. These elements and others may bond as if they were destined to that one place on the page and no other. The total effect, which is admittedly uncommon, is that of a work of literary art that bestows a certain scale we had never before witnessed. We might even borrow the words of Winnie Richards, the neurochemist in DeLillo's *White Noise,* who describes the drug Dylar in the following way: "It's like a galaxy that you can hold in your hand, only more complex, more mysterious" (189).

A first novel's illusion of artistic maturity or artistic creation most often conceals years of anonymous study and difficult labor. Prior to becoming an "author," a person simply must write without the promise of any such achievement. At times a writer has studied the craft and business of writing for a considerable period, all the while experimenting with different methods and forms, communicating with editors and publishers, learning the business, and all while working toward some numinous end. William Faulkner published a book of poetry prior to publishing his first novel; Toni Morrison worked as an educator and editor for years before her first novel was printed. Even after the author has served a long apprenticeship, producing an accomplished, well-reviewed, and lasting first novel is a rare thing. A first novel can fairly be said to anticipate a writer's later achievements only so long as the writer in question continues writing. A writer who continues writing and also lives up to or exceeds a first novel's potential or achievement is a scarce and seemingly fortunate creature.

With these considerations in mind, it would be fair to say that Don DeLillo's *Americana* (1971) is a remarkably accomplished first novel. Reading it today, one has the impression that its writer is a versatile and serious novelist who has not squandered the first effort. This is not to suggest it is without fault or that it entirely anticipates the famed clarity and cohesion of his later fiction. Nonetheless, it can be said to offer a preview of it, and more so than some of his other novels of the 1970s. Reviewing *Americana* in 1971, Joyce Carol Oates (who was then a young novelist, too) noted that "DeLillo is to be congratulated for having accomplished one of the most compelling and sophisticated of 'first novels' that I have ever read."[2] By one standard—the consistency and subtlety of its experimental narration—*Americana* certainly anticipates the later novels. To borrow Oates's term, this is primarily due to how it offers the reader a "sophisticated" narrative structure that immediately suggests DeLillo's mission: to tell two stories at once. The first is the "plot," and the second is a story about how the narrator relates that same plot. (DeLillo critic David Cowart used cinematic terms to describe the effect as "diegetic.")[3] Some refer to this technique as "metafiction," a term describing a style of literary writing that invites the reader to consider literature ironically as artifice commenting on its own making. In a sense, it asks a reader to work on two levels: to follow and enjoy a story and simultaneously to appreciate, think about, and take pleasure from artful exposition of *how* it is made.

Americana

Americana is narrated by its main character, David Bell. David is a rising young talent in the broadcast media, where he writes and directs television programs. David narrates the novel at an unspecified date from an island off the coast of Africa. The reader is never entirely sure why David goes there, and the inattentive reader may become confused by the digressions, flashbacks, and even the minor anachronisms that David uses to tell his story (and perhaps to conceal his tracks). Simultaneously uncomfortable and intimate, David's narration suggests the paradoxical moods that are a trademark of DeLillo's later literary fiction. Comedy competes in it with violence, and parody with nostalgia. These contradictions also describe the novel's narration, which is simultaneously distant (an effect often achieved by David's use of a motion picture camera, and a third layer, in which he describes the film he has made) yet also near (particularly in the flashback scenes). DeLillo disperses this narrative structure over the course of the novel like a scaffold that holds the plot together. We are intended to see the works.

In addition to contrasting narrative moods, *Americana* also previews other features of DeLillo's later novels. Its characters are obtuse yet familiar and always observant of detail. Discursions on history, media, disaster, and language, elements cherished by readers of his later fiction, are also present, if not always to the effect we find them in later writings.[4] There is also a strong temptation, particularly in the early "network" chapters of the novel, to read the novel as a thinly veiled autobiography that DeLillo refined from his years of postgraduate work in the business of commercial advertising. The temptation is substantial and the context true, yet to indulge in biographical criticism is to risk overlooking how the novel portrays a terse romance between American business and American art (a romance whose tension is conveyed in *Americana* by David's alternately cinematic and literary narration).[5]

The culture of American business is a context we find in many of DeLillo's later works, culminating perhaps with the startling novel *Cosmopolis* (2003). It is an interest that begins with *Americana.* David Bell is a descendant of a pioneering family of American television advertising executives, and his genealogy offers him an "insider's view" of the business (and one that he increasingly tries to mediate, using film, as if to turn the medium against itself). His narration is divided into four parts containing a total of twelve individual chapters. The narration combines descriptive prose with long sequences of dialogue, like a film that combines montage with mise-en-scène. As is more often the case in later works, there is some overlap in the relationship between characters and the media; for example, a line from a television commercial migrates to a character's dialogue in the novel. Despite such recursive moments, several significant flashbacks, and the fact that we are never quite sure about the future from which David narrates the book, the novel is generally linear in its chronology as it follows events in David's life over a period of several months during which he leaves the media business.

Part 1 of the novel contains five chapters. The setting is largely preoccupied with David's New York City network office and social life, where he occasionally discusses his family and youth in the fictional town of Old Holly, New York, his college years in California, and the early days of his failed marriage in New York City. The main story line concerns David's career. An emergent star in network programming, he recently produced a television show entitled "Soliloquy," which was cancelled after a short-lived success. As the novel begins, he is planning a new documentary about the Native American Navajo tribe.

Two trademarks of DeLillo's narrative technique appear in these first five chapters. The first is DeLillo's uncanny sense of comedic timing when writing dialogue between characters. Vernacular speech often combines with technical jargon in scenes such as the following, where three of David's colleagues (and rivals) trade ideas with and massage the ego of a network executive named Weede Deney:

> "Apropos of Grace Tully," Joyner said, "I have it on good authority that back in the old days she used to make it with some of the biggest names on the coast. Both coasts, in fact."

> "Let's get together," Weede said. "What I want to know at this juncture is whether the World War III idea is any more viable than it was a week ago in the light of the recent developments on the international scene."
>
> "At this juncture," Richter James said, "the World War III idea is about forty percent less viable than it was a week ago."
>
> "That's what I wanted to know."
>
> "What I want to know," Walter Faye said, "is why we can't show the toilet bowl in the effects-of-solitude prison thing." (72)

DeLillo combines colloquial speech ("prison thing") with caricatures of technical jargon ("forty percent less viable") to elaborate the boardroom style. Thomas DiPietro has aptly described DeLillo's "work as a mystery, born of a street-level love of language and sensitivity to images," and DiPietro's hyphenated phrase certainly describes the characterization of the meeting-room conversation.[6] The scene consists only of dialogue, after all, thereby emphasizing the intonations of the characters' speech (as when Richter James parrots Weede's "at this juncture" phrase) and isolating the careless masculinity of their expressions. In addition, the paratactic and ironically repetitive dialogue spoken by DeLillo's characters, seen here in an early form, often uses linguistic contrast to comedic ends. In this we hear the influence of novelists such as Heller, Pynchon, and Vonnegut, whom literary critics disparagingly described during the 1960s as "Black Humor" writers (a phrase that does not indicate the linguistic variety that is often the basis of dialogue in their works). In DeLillo's breakthrough novel *White Noise,* this style of dialogue is refined to unprecedented effect, combining side-splitting vernacular humor with delicate reflections on the random, mortal consequences of human disasters. It should be noted that DeLillo is a perfectionist about such matters, so much so that he removed certain passages from *Americana* before Penguin reprinted the novel in 1989.[7]

Following the intimate and comedic merging of common speech with boardroom jargon, DeLillo's second achievement in the early chapters of *Americana* is that the novel conveys a sharp contrast between the narrator and his environment. The result is not merely comic or technical: by stressing David's narrative distance, it imbues the novel with philosophical distance and affect. In the passage above, David's narrative remove brings the absurd details of the business culture into focus, a technique that David Cowart rightly notes belongs to an earlier school of American and European fiction concerned with the "alienation" of young (mostly male) characters.[8] While it functions here to comic ends, that same distance will later be the source of more sober reflection. Slowly but surely, David drifts along this initial detachment and out of the world of business. This inexorable motion, which continues outside the frame of the book through some unknown locale and date, begins with these simple observations on the interpersonal dynamics of office culture. The comedy eventually dissolves and gives way to a story about David's more sincere artistic ambitions, and a more serious novel.

The novel expresses David's metaphorical distance in these early chapters as a motion through space. This is typical of DeLillo's fiction, wherein novels that begin in the eastern United States then journey westward, leaving behind the conventional postmodern milieu of the cities to enter rural, desert, or suburban spaces (see, for example, his 1978 novel *Running Dog*). At the end of part 1, David and two friends—Pike and Sullivan—leave New York City. Pike is a business owner and an older man who hangs around David's younger crowd. Sullivan is a sculptor with a studio on the west side of Greenwich Village; she and David have an implied romantic attachment. They leave together to pick up a camper from Bobby Brand, a Vietnam veteran and aspiring novelist who lives in Maine, with the intention of driving it to the Arizona location where David is expected to shoot his documentary. The novel shifts here from a parody of American business to a road novel, with David occasionally reminding the reader that he is narrating from an indeterminate place and slightly more specific time. (Some critics argue that the novel's implicit date of narration is the year 1999.) As the movement begins, it is as though the reader were simultaneously traveling across geographic space and literary genres (the latter effect becoming more pronounced in his subsequent novel, *End Zone*).

Part 2 of *Americana* deviates from the friends' trip into a single long and fragmentary chapter. It starts with David narrating from the island in the future and continues through a series of flashbacks. Most of these depict his hometown of Old Holly. A series of vignettes, each describing a friend, family member, or event in David's life, unspool over the chapter's course. Cinematic techniques begin to emerge as narrative devices. For instance, the chapter's first page suggests he is projecting and watching a film on his island; on the last page, David and his sister Jane watch television commercials with their father on a projector in the basement of the family's home.

While part 2 of the novel implicitly moves forward (David is narrating from the future, but may be watching footage shot on the road trip to Arizona) and backward (David's youth), part 3, which consist of five chapters, returns to the four friends' cross-country journey (Bobby Brand decides to join them). A second deviation takes place when the characters stop in a small midwestern town named Fort Curtis. (It is implied to be close to Chicago, yet it is presumably a fictional town, although there is a historic military fort named Fort Curtis in Arcadia, Missouri.) Anachronistic and quaint, Fort

Curtis seems like a Norman Rockwell painting come alive. David recognizes in it the vestige of his small-town youth in Old Holly. He abandons his documentary project. The turn is sudden but plausible: David was impulsive and unpredictable as a student filmmaker in college. In addition, he cannot resist using cinematic terms to describe himself and his life. Because the town resonates with him in powerful ways, he decides to use his equipment to make an experimental, autobiographical film using residents as doubles for people in his New York family and life. To quote the collegiate football player who is the narrator in DeLillo's subsequent novel *End Zone,* David wishes "to remake memory as a work of art" (70).

In part 3 David recruits townspeople to act in his film. They include a hardware store owner who fought in the Pacific battles of World War II (as did David's father). David recruits the veteran's son as well as an aspiring male actor and his girlfriend, who works in the local community center. Combining random street footage of the town with carefully staged interviews in the local hotel room he has modified, David's film re-creates scenes from his Mount Holly youth, with the actors playing the parts of David, his ex-wife, his father, and so on. In this way part 3 of *Americana* shows David making an experimental film about his own life, or at least his memory of it, as the film he makes in part 3 comments upon the vignettes he narrated in part 2. David's film eventually consumes him. He leaves the broadcast network. The film drives the friends apart. Bobby and Sullivan are revealed to be carrying on an affair, and they return east with Pike. David continues west with his film reels; he is dislocated, a drifter in time and space.

Like part 2 of the novel, part 4 consists of a single long chapter. (DeLillo frequently alternates long chapters in his novels with sequences of shorter ones, bringing to mind the cinematic distinction between montage and mise-en-scène.) In this chapter, David continues traveling west, where instead of finding meaning he descends into a violent and dystopian world. Picked up by Clevenger (a man who sells auto parts around the Southwest and owns a race-car track in Texas), David crosses the Plains and the Rockies. Landscapes reminiscent of Nabokov's *Lolita* appear: they are littered with motels, truck stops, and communes inspired by science fiction. Everything appears vulnerable, transient. The novel's weird hilarity and cinematic nostalgia turn cold, even sinister. In the conclusive scenes, Clevenger hires David to work on his Texas race track. Upon arriving there, a scatological, drunken orgy breaks out among the employees (reminiscent of scenes from *Salò,* Pasolini's infamous and brilliant 1975 film). Leaving the track, David is picked up on the road by a one-armed sailor who threatens to rape him. After escaping to Dealey Plaza in Dallas, David flies back to New York, and the novel ends.

As noted earlier, David narrates the novel from an indeterminate island on an African coast. The fact that he does so implies an additional movement, from New York across the Atlantic. Hence, David's age and location at the time of the novel's narration are not entirely clear. Along the way, the attentive reader will pick up clues to David's age and the years of events that take place in the novel. We know he was divorced at the age of twenty-three, and that at one point he refers to himself in the past tense as having been twenty-nine years of age; at other points he is twenty-seven years old, and thirty. The disorienting, anachronistic effect defers David's story to a future from which David projects his life onto the past. The answer to "When is it set?" may very well be "Here and now" on an endless loop. The answer is not as important as the means by which the question is posed. DeLillo clearly uses cinema as a trope to frame literary narrative, and the novel is always indicating its own construction through David's cinematic narration. As a metafiction, *Americana* offers a strong early example of DeLillo's interest in combining and adapting techniques from different arts. One might even call it mixed media, were it not for the fact that its primary medium is linguistic.

Hence DeLillo regards the blank page as a sort of narrative surrogate for the film screen. On it David projects his life. The effect is augmented by the doubling features of David's film, which seeks to visualize the novel. Peter Boxall recently noted in a lucid summary of the matter: "The idea that animates David's film . . . is that one might use this power [of the motion picture camera] to produce a new kind of autobiography that transfigures one's life rather than simply recording it. David is imagining here a new version of Proust's *À la recherche du temps perdu* (1913–1927) that uses the annihilating power of the camera in the place of the recuperative power of narrative."[9]

Boxall's comments sum up the matter, but they also raises a difficult question that appears frequently in readings of DeLillo's fiction: is DeLillo a late modernist, or a postmodernist who recycles literary modernism in the way that a sculptor might recycle everyday objects into "found art"? DeLillo's use of modernist narrative techniques and how he incorporates cinematic elements into his fiction constitutes a field of extensive literary inquiry, and not only in the study of DeLillo's works. When a character refers to Joyce's *Finnegans Wake* in *Americana,* critics prompt readers to consider the author's influences on DeLillo (and call on DeLillo's citation of those influences to support the claim). The matter at hand involves source studies but only to a limited degree. (A character invokes Charles Dickens in *White Noise,* but no one would cite Dickens as a major influence on DeLillo's fiction.) The more prominent question that arises in such moments is that of whether DeLillo's "embrace of a modernist avant-garde," as Philip Nel calls it, can be regarded as an extension of modernism or whether it falls under the postmodern predilection for "recycling" elements of previous cultures (in this case, literary modernism of the first half of the twentieth century, including but not limited to writers such as Proust and Joyce).[10]

Irrespective of varied positions on the matter, the critical debate surrounding modernism and postmodernism in *Americana* nonetheless illuminates how David, his film, and the novel itself inhabit a world in which people, art, and business have become unmoored. Drifting in and through genre, history, and memory, DeLillo's *Americana* ambitiously attempts to render that very same motion into something artful. It does not suggest a concession to the disruptive forces that shape contemporary American life but, rather, a willful attempt to render those forces into aesthetic forms that would affirm that art and the artist might work in critical relation to a time-bending and dislocating consumerism. This is true even in the lighter early chapters of the novel, where DeLillo's focus is fixed on the dialogue of interpersonal capitalism. There is always a serious intonation in those scenes whereby not only persons but also office machines (elevators, mimeographs, telephones), office décor (coffee tables), and even entire city neighborhoods (Gramercy Park, Greenwich Village) carry a hidden and elusive significance. David senses it, seeks it out, and discovers in his attempt to find it (through cinematic re-creations of his memory) that wild, dangerous relics (memories, outcasts, drifters) inhabit the spaces between such objects, and that he too has become one of those things. Whether considering office décor, characters, idyllic small towns, or sprawling, opulent cities, *Americana* is very much a novel about a young man who attempts to make his art at a remove from the absurdity of American business culture. DeLillo's later novels will not be so diffident as *Americana* with respect to that relationship. It should be noted, however, that *Americana* stands apart from its precursors in literary fiction about American business. Certainly, it shares Sinclair Lewis's eye for small-town detail and combines it with Jon Dos Passos's penchant for using narrative techniques borrowed from cinema. Yet it departs from those traditions in significant ways. It combines technical and profane variants of American speech as if to provide a new language for a new form of capitalism, a parlance suited for the staccato frenzy of a society moving away from small-business commerce and even large corporations into an age of ephemeral information and images. In that emergent world, slogans and sound bites jump into the consciousness without source or warning. They colonize memory and distort history, personal or otherwise. In trying to detach himself from that world, David Bell would appear to seek, perhaps naively, a sanctuary in the cinema, only to find it ironically in the novel.

If our hypothetical bookstore patron were to continue reading DeLillo's subsequent novels of the 1970s, that reader would encounter many of the strands developed or introduced by *Americana*. Characters will continue to offer commentary on how media technologies alter literary-narrative experience and art in general (although not always using the cinematic techniques that structure David's narration in opposition to the world of television advertising). By different means the goal would be the same: characters in DeLillo's novels would seek what Frank Lentricchia later described as "the desire for a universal third person" that suggests a "new self because a new world."[11] While individual characters in DeLillo's fiction might not ever attain the perspective of that universal third person, our reader would move closer to it, as each of DeLillo's novels would provide new, increasingly kaleidoscopic narratives of the relations between people, words, and things, relations by and against which we measure the spectrum of contemporary experience.

End Zone

Don DeLillo's second novel is entitled *End Zone* (1972). Where *Americana* might have appealed to the cineaste and the reader of experimental fiction, *End Zone* appealed, at least on its surface, to another audience: the sports fan interested in genre fiction. On the one hand, it extends many of the elements of *Americana*. First, it has obvious structural similarities. It is divided into three parts, with the first and third parts sectioned into short chapters; the middle part, a centerpiece of sorts, consists of a single long chapter. (We find the same tripartite structure in the later *White Noise*.) Second, it resembles its predecessor in that it is narrated by a young man. Here he is named Gary Harkness, and like David Bell, he hails from a small town in upstate New York. Gary also seeks to define himself by a combination of activities—in this case, collegiate football and academic life.

Third, the novel takes place and is narrated from the present time, and it is very much attuned to world events beyond the immediate frame of its action (perhaps more so than *Americana*). It is primarily set in a small college town in the American Southwest (and not unlike the college that David attended in *Americana*). More so than *Americana*, *End Zone* uses that context to survey social conflicts in American culture. These include race relations, class difference, gender inequality, and the ideological and military contests of the Cold War. Perhaps more than any of these, it is a novel about American youth during the final, brutal years of the Vietnam War. In these ways *End Zone* moves through the culture, as did *Americana,* but at a more urgent pace.

In other important ways, *End Zone* is completely unlike *Americana* in that it is perhaps the most generic of DeLillo's novels. In the first place, it belongs to the genre of the campus novel (a uniquely modern genre tied to an era of more accessible higher education, but also an offshoot of the bildungsroman, or coming-of-age novel). As such, it is a novel about Gary and his social circle in the small Texas campus of Logos College. A self-conscious and self-defined "exile," Gary gravitates towards and befriends other characters who live on the margins of that small college world. The novel devotes more attention to ancillary characters than did *Americana,* thereby creating a narrative that at times resembles a faux-sociological case study of American college youth. Characters include Gary's roommate and teammate Anatole Bloomberg, a young Jewish American man who wishes to "unjew" himself so as to become "super rational" and "non-ethnic" (186). There is also Myna, an overweight young white woman and devotee of science fiction, who later loses weight and changes her appearance to adapt to social norms. There is Robinson Taft, an African American football recruit, who reluctantly plays the role of the athletic star (and with whom Gary rarely speaks). A tertiary cast includes a host of student athletes whose pastimes include ribald, scatological parties, absurd discussions of intellectual matters, and maniacal locker room gossip. Rounding out the cast are two college instructors—Major Staley and Alan Zapalac—as well as several football coaches. Major Staley teaches a course on the history of air power and leads the campus Air Force ROTC. Zapalac teaches exobiology, a popular course in which he gives thoughtful, rambling lectures that often turn to personal anecdotes. Whereas Major Staley is somewhat aloof, Zapalac is gregarious. Ever sensitive to the physical world, Zapalac recognizes that his students have invented a kind of figural antimatter: a student who does not exist, yet nonetheless takes tests, answers roll call, and the like. Zapalac allows the prank. Major Staley simulates war games in his hotel room; Zapalac rambles on subjects ranging from theology to organ transplants. Over the course of roughly six months that begin in late summer and end during the early spring college term, Gary socializes with this cast, seeking an identity or an epiphany, as must all young characters in a campus novel.

In all this *End Zone* may appear unremarkable. Indeed, it may even seem antithetical to the cerebral moods and wild narrative experiments of *Americana.* DeLillo's contemporaries, as well as his later readers, did not take well to it. In an early review, Nelson Algren described *End Zone* as having betrayed the promise of *Americana.* Later critics imposed an allegorical interpretation on the novel. In a 2011 study Paul Giaimo argued that *End Zone* is a veiled "anti-war" novel in that it uses the culture of college football to illustrate how a culture of conflict erodes and finally destroys its narrator's ability to think in an ethical way. In Giaimo's thesis, the novel asks: if the world is going to end in nuclear holocaust, of what use is morality?[12] A grim critical reputation precedes and reinforces Giaimo's point. Daniel Aaron argued that the novel's narrator is a figure of "catastrophe" and his football coach belongs among "Sherwood Anderson's sad grotesques."[13]

Allegory requires another text—something outside itself to which it refers (such as the Vietnam War or Winesburg, Ohio). Other critics such as Tom LeClair, an important DeLillo critic and one of DeLillo's first academic champions among academics, described *End Zone* as a form of "polar fiction."[14] In this way, LeClair does not interpret the characters in an allegorical manner. Rather, he notes the function of genre in DeLillo's novel. In an oft-cited interview with DeLillo, Anthony DeCurtis called *End Zone* a novel of "alienation," a keyword that invokes the modern tradition (one hesitates to call it a genre) of literary fiction inspired by European writers and existential philosophy. In this way we are reminded of the earlier discussion of the role of modernism in DeLillo's writing. And we ask, what could writers such as Kafka, Sartre, or Camus have to do with a campus novel about an American football player? To further complicate the matter, in that very same interview by DeCurtis, DeLillo describes *End Zone* as a book "about extreme places and extreme states of mind." In making the claim, DeLillo noted that *End Zone* "wasn't about football."[15]

Yet *End Zone* is very much a novel about football. As we shall see, it revels in particular in the language, as well as in the visual kinesis, of the televised sport. DeLillo's denial of the novel's subject points the reader away from a literal, generic reading of *End Zone* as a novel belonging to yet another genre: the sports novel. Ironically, it is a book that has found a following among readers of American sports fiction, and one might argue that its long middle chapter is the best ever written about a college football game. (A section of the book was reprinted in the April 17, 1972, issue of *Sports Illustrated.*) By turning away from its subject matter, we risk overlooking DeLillo's remarkable capacity for writing literary fiction about American sports, a talent he has developed over the course of a long career of writing on baseball and football as well as on ancillary economic activities such as sports betting. One could make a convincing case that there is not a single writer of contemporary literary fiction who writes about American sports in a manner that even approximates DeLillo's originality and inventiveness, and furthermore that DeLillo's literary writing about sports paved the way for writers of a later generation to engage the subject. One has only to consider David Foster Wallace's celebrated "tennis" novel *Infinite Jest* (1996), the best-selling work that made Wallace into a literary superstar, to recognize the consequence of Gary Harkness's "catastrophe."

End Zone also introduces elements of great import to DeLillo's later fiction. Foremost among those elements is the "crowd." It appears in the stands, at the edges of Gary's perception, or in implicit forms (as when the reader follows a radio broadcast of the big game, a broadcast that places the reader in the listening audience, if not necessarily the stands near the field itself). The figure would take more substantial form in DeLillo's later fiction where the dynamics of spectatorship venture close to replicating the fragmented perspectives of Cubist painting. In *Mao II,* a confused mother and father watch from the crowd as their daughter participates in the mass wedding organized by a religious cult at Yankee stadium. Later still, the frontispiece to one of the novel's sections reproduces a photograph of fans being crushed against a barrier at a European soccer match. In these instances readers are placed in a position where they are asked to consider how they consume mass culture, how our physical space (a stadium) is organized to enhance (or obscure) that experience, and the role that technology plays in mediating how we watch a game or other event, whether on a broadcast or from the stands.

In the more well-known and well-wrought examples cited above, baseball most often appears as a mass-culture double for modernity. In *End Zone* football appears instead as the postmodern sport par excellence, a game of kinetic televisual power, of fragmented regional rivalries between schools and states, and of the emergent media and marketing juggernaut that translated the collegiate form of the sport to a unified and successful professional league on a national scale during the late 1960s and early 1970s. With these qualities in mind, *End Zone* depicts the game's tactics, strategy, history, and psychology in convincing detail. It would almost seem realistic.

Yet there is also truth in DeLillo's claim that *End Zone* is not "about football." Critics are also right to perceive that the novel exceeds the genre of the sports novel in significant ways. We might ask, if it is not a sports novel, or a campus novel, or a novel about war, then what is it?

As we saw with *Americana,* DeLillo elaborates certain narrative techniques to make literary art. That novel relied on narrative sleights of hand to embellish its narrator's distance. Anachronism, geographic dislocation, and a densely layered narrative perspective (does David Bell's narration provide voice-over, in the form of a novel, to his experimental film?) combine to generate a restless and disaffected mood. They were techniques drawn primarily from cinema. *End Zone* adopts a different technique insofar as its narrative models and experiments work with literary materials. (To be fair, however, DeLillo's cinematic influences never entirely vanish from his fiction.) Understood in this regard, *End Zone*'s subject matter (football) may appear incidental in and of itself, but it is by virtue of its combination with the materials of a second literary genre—the war novel—that *End Zone* marks an important early turn in DeLillo's career insofar as his novels begin to experiment not only with narrative technique but also with the conventions of genre.

This is not to say the DeLillo begins writing within a specific genre. John McClure has published several important essays and book chapters on DeLillo's writings. In an important 1991 essay entitled "Postmodern Romance: Don DeLillo and the Age of Conspiracy," McClure described DeLillo's approach to genre as follows: "DeLillo crafts his fictions out of the forms of popular romance: out of the espionage thriller, the imperial adventure novel, the western, science fiction, even the genre of occult adventure. He may conduct us, in one novel, across several genres."[16] McClure does not discuss *End Zone* in his essay, devoting his attention instead to DeLillo's espionage novels of the late 1970s, yet his description of DeLillo's use of genre applies to the earlier novel insofar as *End Zone* deliberately juxtaposes two specialized languages (those of football and science, and specifically military science). The result is metaphorical, an incongruity of simultaneous genres. In rhetorical terms we might say that *End Zone*'s combined genres elaborate a "symbol" or individual figure of speech at the more level extensive plane of narrative organization. A reader might have inferred as much from the novel's title, with its overt allusion to Samuel Beckett's 1957 play *Endgame,* its English translation referring to the concluding moves of a chess match. DeLillo's title refers both to the literal space of the end zone on a football field—the rectangular space where athletes score touchdowns by crossing a threshold—and also a philosophical plane that Gary, the novel's narrator, ultimately reaches as he crosses the genres of the sports novel, the war novel, the campus novel, and so forth. This is what many of DeLillo's readers refer to as "metafiction," a term that has lost its currency but adequately describes fiction that integrates and comments upon other fictions. In this case and others in DeLillo's career, the point is not merely to combine other genres. In his essay McClure describes how DeLillo's writing seeks "sites within capitalism, and discovers there the materials for new forms of romance."[17]

As with *Americana,* the reader is made conscious of a story being told, but in *End Zone* we are asked also to consider the relationship between genres and tradition, and to do so from the novel's opening lines. For example, when describing the racially charged recruitment and arrival of a star African American college football player named Robinson Taft, Gary tells the reader, "The mansion has long been haunted (double metaphor coming up) by the invisible man" (3). In technical terms, the reference to Ellison's *Invisible Man* (1952) is an allusion and not a metaphor. The "double metaphor" lies instead in the narrative splitting of the text into separate modes: the narrator's parenthetical address to the reader ironically exposes the artifice of the narrative's mixed genres. In this case the immediate matter is not only race relations during the post–civil rights era but the relationship of the sports novel to the African American literary novel. By and through this ironic narration, *End Zone* begins its metalinguistic experiment whereby the juxtaposition of specialized languages functions as a "double metaphor" to reveal some other order of experience that the reader can access through literary fiction. This Brechtian technique in which a narrator addresses both the audience and the artificiality of the art is a common one in postmodern literary writing, and to DeLillo's credit he avoids using it to excess in *End Zone*. The reader is notified from the start, and the novel proceeds.

As noted earlier, the novel's centerpiece is the long chapter that constitutes its second part. In that section, the consequence of the parenthetical aside is amplified to a remarkable scale. The context: in preceding chapters, the Logos College football team has practiced for and played its games with its eye on a single opponent—Centrex, a violent and ruthless team that dominates the sport in the region. This is going to be the "big game," the coaches tell Gary and his teammates, the one that defines them as athletes and young men. As the game begins, the narration places the reader in the crowd: "(The spectator, at this point, is certain to wonder whether he must now endure a football game in print—the author's way of adding his own neat quarter notch to the scarred blue steel of combat writing. The game, after all, is known for its assault-technology motif. . . .)" (111).

Over the course of two pages, the parenthetical passage contains descriptions of future scenes in the novel and commentary on forms of social organization and the role of the spectator (is it the reader, or someone in the crowd?), concluding with affirmation of the "author's permanent duty to unbox the lexicon [of sports "gibberish"] for all eyes to see—a cryptic ticking mechanism in search of a revolution." And then abruptly the paragraph ends, and we hear the quarterback calling a play from the field: "Blue turk right, double-slot, zero snag delay" (113). The cut to the play call at the line of scrimmage returns the narration from the "author" to Gary's point of view. Yet in this heightened view that uses paratactical sentences, as if to split Gary into observer and observed, Gary sees the game but also sees himself in it. The linguistic incongruity of the narration, divided between literary artifice and the juxtaposition of "real" languages, begins to fragment Gary's being. The sudden cuts in the narration, as we jump from dialogue to narration of the action, convey a violent effect: Gary, we sense, is being torn apart, whittled down by repeated blows, and forced into a condition he would refuse.

At one point Gary describes his own play on the field using the third-person narrative voice. In this passage, he adopts the tone of a color commentator in a radio or television broadcast as he calls "a hard earned first down for unspectacular Harkness" (116). There is a comparable visual moment from contemporary American football culture. During the second half of Super Bowl XLIII, Larry Fitzgerald, a wide receiver for the Arizona Cardinals, caught a pass near midfield. He outpaced his defender with a burst of speed and raced toward the end zone; as he did so, he looked up at the large video monitor above the field, thereby watching Larry Fitzgerald make the play. If Fitzgerald's helmet had been equipped with a wireless microphone that was connected to the broadcast booth, and had he called the very play he was making during the live broadcast of the game, we might have something that approximates the divided consciousness of Gary's persona in this scene.

In this scene and others, the narration of *End Zone* splits its narrative perspective into a multiplicity of viewpoints. They are refracted through the prisms of the narrator, the mass media, and the crowd. There is no equivalent scene in *Americana,* although its cinematic narration implies a similar distancing as well as DeLillo's early willingness to experiment with complex modes of storytelling. As was the case in *Americana,* where metacinematic narration provides David with a refuge from commercial art, the metalinguistic narrative in *End Zone* indicates Gary's movement towards an isolated, highly aestheticized form of narrative expression.

As is sometimes the case in DeLillo's novels, that movement is expressed in terms of a search for spiritual significance or mystical revelation. This is true of *End Zone,* as Gary leans increasingly in that direction, yet never seems to escape his secular predicament. Gary's gradual movement away from the football team's social structure takes different forms. They include solitary walks in the desert, visits to Robinson Taft in which the two do not converse, and apocalyptic fantasies in which Gary imagines himself inhabiting an irradiated and ashen postnuclear landscape. Yet these do not provide solace, as Gary finds he is not alone in his condition, and therefore he is not privy to an experience or secret that would differentiate him from others. For instance, some of Gary's teammates and friends express similar thoughts of detachment and escape. Anatole seeks to evade his ethnic identity, regarding assimilation as the best option. Others vanish into the classroom jargon of business and advertising. Myna Corbett, a classmate of Gary's in Alan Zapalac's exobiology class (and Gary's eventual girlfriend for a short time), offers the best example. Myna describes herself as an overweight young woman who wears mismatched clothing to conceal her blotched skin. A science fiction enthusiast, Myna is enchanted by the writings of a fictional Mongolian author named

Tudev Nemkhu. In chapter 20 of the novel, Myna summarizes Nemkhu's writings with eloquence and authority, explaining his sources, characters, and narrative methods. These offer to Myna what Gary thought football would offer to him: an identity and purpose. Myna anticipates later women characters in DeLillo's works who perceive male characters with a rigorous and critical independence of mind. Few critics have defended DeLillo against the claim that his characters are superficial (meaning that they lack realistic psychological "depth"). Tom LeClair makes an exception for Myna in this regard: "In her final confrontation with Gary, Myna previews these later figures, although she suffers the same malaise as does Gary during the 'science fiction' phase that constitutes the majority of her role in the novel."[18]

In the end Myna finds a role to play when Gary cannot, and she remains in what we might best describe, given the novel's obvious models in modern French art, a *malaise*. The French term does not translate well into English from the French. In Latinate languages it connotes an illness in one's essence, an existential imbalance of sorts. The pathological "disease," vaguely medieval "ill-humor," or the casual "ill-at-ease" do not suffice to capture the word's philosophical connotations. The French term is used often in English, however, even if its ontological connotation, which communicates a disruption in one's being or "essence," is sometimes lost. The term nonetheless describes Gary's mood as the novel proceeds: it is the "end" to which his divided narration works over the novel's course. Yes, we must admit, *End Zone* is not a novel "about football"; it is instead a novel about language and specifically how specialized languages—jargon, acronyms, diagrams—limit experience, imagination, and history, forcing them into spaces they cannot occupy without becoming restless, withdrawn, and degraded. Try as he might, Gary cannot find a way out. DeLillo described the ultimate effect in his 1982 interview with Tom LeClair: "Some of the characters [in *End Zone*] have a made-up nature. They are pieces of jargon. They engage in wars of jargon with each other. There is a mechanical element, a kind of fragmented self-consciousness. I took this further in *Ratner's Star*."[19]

Hope rests with art, or at least its potential to illuminate and reinvent the language we use to narrate a human experience. In dramatizing jargon and specialized language, giving it a physical form as a character, for instance, DeLillo's novels do not merely give themselves up to the overdeterminations of technical variants of American English. For example, in *Americana* DeLillo deferred a good deal of the novel's narrative responsibility to the conventions of film, but the strategy had a reciprocal effect in that it provided David with a new way to narrate his own biography. One might also take the positive view and note that despite Gary's bleak prospects, *End Zone* confidently acknowledges language as its primary medium, and in it we see DeLillo expanding his craft as a writer by placing the narrative burden on language rather than a cinematic substitute. Take, for example, the trademark "lists" that appear briefly in *Americana* and become a more coherent presence in *End Zone.* In the latter novel they assume the mantric qualities recognized by readers of DeLillo's later novels. Characters recite words rather than speak; slogans appear randomly, without warning, as if commercialism had combined at some genetic level with religious faith.

In these instances DeLillo's literary fiction does not merely "mimic" language in order to make it real. In the case of the mantric slogans or euphemisms that constitute specialized jargon, *End Zone* illuminates the dehumanizing and corrosive force of language, and Gary embodies its existential effect. While we recognize its abjection and despair, we also begin to note the absurdity and comedy of contemporary American English. In this way the movement of characters through a metalinguistic narrative space is allegorical in that it approximates the reader's movement through the novel's language. It is a physical experience of the texture of words. At one point early in the novel, Gary speaks to Anatole Bloomberg in his dorm room, and describes the matter as follows: "Words move the body into position. In time the position itself dictates events. As the sun went down I tried to explain this concept to Bloomberg" (45). As the novel proceeds, however, Gary cannot escape the idea that this movement is a trap; the reader, placed in a position to consider the novel as artifice as well as art, may see it otherwise, as a state of being we can endure and even enjoy.

Purists might resent DeLillo's attempt to transpose the high-modern style of Beckett and Brecht to the idiom of American sports culture. Ambition has seldom had allies in history; perhaps the risk exceeds the reward. Yet from *End Zone* through *White Noise,* DeLillo's novels would increasingly render and comment upon the specialized variants of American English (football, military intelligence, pop music, mathematics, and so on). Like a mad lexicographer, DeLillo would expose their pretense in combination with their generic narrative forms (such as the sports novel, the spy novel, and the disaster novel) so as to reconfigure the reader's relationship to literary fiction. One might recognize in this type of experimentalism the optimism of a generation seeking alternatives to convention. Like the protagonists of these early novels, the novelist decrypts contemporary words, logos, and signals. While there is irony and experiment, comedy and violence, there is also urgency and a forward-looking sensibility in DeLillo's early fiction. It is not so much concerned with revising the past as it is with working through the present towards some goal that is beyond the reach of the very languages he must use to attain it.

Over time the urgency of that mission would take new forms in DeLillo's activism on behalf of imprisoned writers, the emergence of "history" as a more complex subject in his writing and the eventual diminishing of overt "metanarrative" strategies in favor of a more poetic narrative sensibility. That trajectory may very well begin with the grim finality of *End Zone,* a novel whose linguistic incongruities would extend to other narrative forms and moods in DeLillo's subsequent novels of the 1970s.

Great Jones Street

Don DeLillo published six novels during the period 1971–78. In chronological order, these were *Americana* (1971), *End Zone* (1972), *Great Jones Street* (1973), *Ratner's Star* (1976), *Players* (1977), and *Running Dog* (1978). As noted, *Americana* and *End Zone* are characterized by the plasticity of DeLillo's narrative style. Of the first two novels, *End Zone* is more representative of the four remaining novels of this period. In the first place, its metalinguistic sensibility permits DeLillo to combine variants of American English in unique ways, a quality generally found in his novels of the 1970s. In the second place, the novels betray a heightened and increasingly refined sense of how to combine genres. Whereas *End Zone* awkwardly combined the sports novel and the campus novel, later novels would combine genres with greater ease. Cinematic analogy may serve to make the point: DeLillo would become like the American film director Howard Hawks, who made excellent films in all the major narrative genres of his time. The later novels would show that DeLillo could clearly elaborate the expected conventions of a single genre, move from one genre to another, and combine them in a single novel with deliberate ease.

"Pastiche" is the term sometimes used by literary critics to describe this technique. In this view DeLillo does not "reinvent" genres by adding new elements to them (as, say, Hammett or Chandler transformed the classical detective from genteel Victorian into a street-hardened tough). Rather, in pastiche we find the recycling of older forms (such as genres). The term does not describe a new genre; for instance, a genre such as "steampunk," which combines Victorian science with a twentieth-century pop sensibility, is a type of pastiche, but pastiche is not in itself a genre. It is a mode of composition, in the literal sense of the term, resulting in a composite work of art. It may contain elements of older generic forms in a nongeneric work, or, as in the case of steampunk, take on the attributes of a "new" genre. Pastiche suffices to some extent as a descriptor of DeLillo's novels, the exception being that they contain an essayistic or discursive element similar to that found in the films of Jean-Luc Godard.

In addition to the physical assembly of the metafictional narrative, pastiche has an affective sense. Critics generally consider nostalgia to be the primary emotional register of pastiche. Nostalgia results from the recovery of old forms whereby the reader or viewer experiences a sense of history (or its absence). It is unlike the Romantic obsession with classical ruins, whereby the observer was meant to experience the languid passing of historical time. History does not seem to pass in the same way in pastiche, if at all. Rather, the emotional effect may be akin to being trapped, or frozen in time. It is history without future or past. Genres, literary forms with set conventions that communicate a kind of narrative architecture, offer the artist the ideal plane for experiment. When Gary Harkness narrates a combined campus/sports novel in *End Zone,* he appears not only as a young person trying to avoid the impositions of language, but he is also attempting to avoid the identities that are consequent to those impositions. Anatole strives to become a gentile, Myna gives in to the pressure to conform, but for some reason Gary cannot follow convention. Like a work of art frozen in a timeless state that has no future or past, he is caught between conformity to tradition and a future alternative that will not appear to him. Encased in genre, he refuses to become generic.

Pastiche, nostalgia, and genre do not, however, fully explain the result that DeLillo achieves with the novels that follow *End Zone.* In those modes, anachronism functions as a weak substitute for history. In DeLillo, by contrast, the anachronism of a genre's persistent vitality and relevance becomes part of the narrative form. One might say that DeLillo's genres are not merely dead forms that we recycle into new combinations. They function instead as histories of the present time. Readers and critics have often used the term "paranoia" to describe the result. But whether it is Thomas Pynchon's parody of Richard Hofstadter's famous study *The Paranoid Style in American Politics* (1964) in Pynchon's own *The Crying of Lot 49* (1966) or whether it is the post-JFK culture of "conspiracy theory" that DeLillo skillfully avoided in his novel *Libra,* the term paranoia does not ever fully capture a well-written novel's ability to combine generic elements so as to escape, and even ridicule, the cataleptic, hopeless consequences of pastiche. One might point to the "open-ended" conclusions of DeLillo's novels of this period (the "conclusion" of his 1978 novel *Running Dog* comes to mind) as a means by which they avoid the "trap" that closed *End Zone.*

DeLillo's third novel, *Great Jones Street* (1973), exemplifies how the rather academic matters described above are useful in helping us understand DeLillo's fiction, if only to a point. Like its predecessor, *Great Jones Street* is a novel about language. Its plot revolves around a drug known as "the product" that disrupts the human brain's ability to coordinate words. And as in

Americana, the novel's protagonist is a creative artist living in New York City and negotiating a world of mass media (in this way, *Great Jones Street* approximates also the Warholesque sensibility of DeLillo's later *Mao II,* in that it is concerned with the media culture of celebrity). The artist in question is named Bucky Wunderlick, a rock star who has suddenly left his bandmates in the middle of a concert tour. Bucky has retreated into private life only to be drawn into a plot in which a number of competing individuals and organizations force him to hold "the product" even as they compete with one another to analyze it, obtain it, and synthesize it for mass distribution and sale. In this way DeLillo combines elements of other genres—the mystery, the thriller—into a narrative that resembles something "new." This effect may result from the cohesion of the different genres that constitute *Great Jones Street* (a sure sign of DeLillo's growing expertise as a writer). It may also be attributed to DeLillo's increasingly sophisticated ability to depict the subtle forces that shape the present time, as if genres and history were not dead ends but apertures. Regardless of the cause, there is a decisive turn in *Great Jones Street,* a novel that marks a turning point in the narrative strategies that constitute the fundamental work of DeLillo's literary career.

Contemporary literary scholar Florence Dore has recently offered a thesis that helps explain DeLillo's *Great Jones Street.* Looking back over recent American literary fiction, she defines a "new subgenre" that she calls the "rock novel," one whose mature form appears after the year 2000.[20] Novelists working in this mode (Jonathan Lethem is her primary example) combine elements of popular music and blues-derived rock and roll. Conventions include song lyrics and allusions to musicians, as well as visual elements of music commodities such as the liner notes to a compact disc or the covers of vinyl records (features that appear in *Great Jones Street* in the form of the lyric sheet and the music-industry press release). Placing the genre in a historical context, Dore invokes Ian Watt's famous discussion of the "private orientation" of the modern novel. (Here one might also recall Georg Lukacs's contention that the novel confirms the "inner life" of the modern subject.) Dore argues that "rather than simply killing off the novel, contemporary American novelists who make use of rock and roll preserve the genre, update it to make it suitable for life in the twenty-first century. Rock novelists revivify the novel by reanimating, precisely, 'private experience.'"[21]

Dore notes *Great Jones Street* as an important precursor to the subgenre she defines, and it is useful to recall that DeLillo's novel engages the matter of privacy in contemporary American life (and implicitly, the novel's function). The novel introduces the matter by way of a minor character named Skippy, who represents the "Happy Valley Commune," an experimental group who seek to recruit the novel's protagonist as a symbol of their movement (and also as an accomplice to their theft of "the product"). In an early scene, Skippy defines the group's mission as that of "returning the idea of privacy to American life" (17). Bucky, the novel's protagonist, has recently abandoned a public career as a musician and retreated into a quasi-monastic seclusion. That seclusion is continuously interrupted, however, by agents who seek to drag him back into the media spotlight or use his celebrity to some other end. In his first interview (given to Tom LeClair in 1982), DeLillo replied to LeClair's question about the novel in the following terms: "I think rock music is a music of loneliness and isolation. The Doors work very well at the beginning of *Apocalypse Now.* A man with a half-shattered mind, alone in a rented room. Noise, excess, electricity, Vietnam—all these things are tied together in *Great Jones Street,* and a certain tension is drawn out of the hero's silence, his withdrawal. Bucky Wunderlick's music moves from political involvement to extreme self-awareness to childlike babbling."[22] It is then useful to regard this generic element of *Great Jones Street* as one that confirms the novel's orientation towards individual subjectivity.

As such, Dore's argument defines a genre of writing that is missing from the spectrum of LeClair's "polar fiction" that I discussed in the previous section. There I described how *End Zone* initiated DeLillo's turn to writing in and about genres, whereby he combined them so as to achieve the "metafictional" effects that typify his work of the 1970s. The key feature there was that of a metaphorical incongruity inflated to narrative scale. At that narrative level, the inward-looking gravitation of *Great Jones Street* finds its counterpoint in a kind of centrifugal, public motion: a movement through private life yet always away from it into the sphere of public life, language, and history. On the novel's opening page, that motion is described as "the circumstance of one man imparting erotic terror to the dreams of the republic" (1). In subsequent novels characters will entertain this possibility and abandon their privacy to venture into a public experience. It is an experience they initially wished to avoid only to find that the public world and its constituent features—historical events, crowds, commerce, language—are entirely different from that which they initially retreated, expected, or imagined. "Paranoia," in the literal sense, is a distracted state of *mind,* but in DeLillo's protagonists in and after *Great Jones Street,* it does not appear so much as a division between "fact" and "fiction" than as a division between the inner life of the individual and that individual's thoughtful interaction with public life.

In this way the narrative features, generic elements, and linguistic incongruities of the earlier novels achieve a more stable and focused form in *Great Jones Street.* When chapters of conventional narrative prose (Bucky's tenuous privacy) give way to excerpts from lyric sheets and press releases (the public, commodified form of Bucky's inner life), the two qualities join to confirm the work of an artist who regards the novel as an experimental form that, to borrow Dore's term, "reanimates" the dramatic condition of the individual in the present time. Most important of all, perhaps, is the fact that DeLillo will use the novel as a literary form to dramatize, elaborate, and affirm its urgency and relevance. This line of thinking would seem to culminate in the character of Bill Gray in *Mao II* (1991), but it continues through DeLillo's fiction as well as his role as a public artist and intellectual. The latter includes his activism on behalf of persecuted writers and his work among patients with Alzheimer's disease, but it also appears in dozens of important characters and scenes throughout his later writings (and not only in novels). These are amplified by the gregarious reticence of his interviews and the somber performances of his readings and other public appearances. In sum, it is useful to regard the characters, concerns, and generic features of *Great Jones Street* as offering a glimpse for the first time of DeLillo's later career as a novelist and also as an involved citizen and public advocate of the arts. If one were to listen for some biographical tension at the fiction's core, this dynamic exchange between private and public life, an exchange that is dramatized by the narrative plasticity of the early novels, and *Great Jones Street* in particular, would seem a better conduit for it than would allusion, setting, or fictional character.

On its surface, *Great Jones Street* is characterized by a casual style. Its idiom is an easy vernacular peppered with elements of music-industry slang. Syntactic ordering of sentences is idiosyncratic at times, with the occasional inverted sentence suggesting an urban, ethnic linguistic scene. Dramatization of character and place is also lucid as other qualities of DeLillo's prose appear in relief against the diminished narrative apparatus. The latter has not been removed but rather integrated into the dramatic elements of the plot. While the characters still observe and comment upon the world (and the plot itself), the narrative distance that typified *Americana* and *End Zone* is no longer a perspective to be attained outside the novel or within it by some movement across space. Here too the role of genre becomes more subtle, as the terse urban vernacular of the modern detective novel is mixed together with the psychedelic jargon of the counterculture, without excessive dramatic contrast (that is, embodiment in characters such as Professor Zapalac and Major Staley in *End Zone*).

Bucky Wunderlick, the reluctant rock star protagonist who narrates the novel, is a more sympathetic and congenial figure than previous narrators, moving the plot along at a leisurely pace. The reader meets principal characters without delay, and the novel begins, as did *Americana,* in media res but without the extensive flashbacks that require the set-up of David's family history or Gary's quixotic travels from one college to another. We meet Globke, Bucky's manager, a self-professed "philosopher of bad taste," and Azarian, Bucky's taciturn and anxious former bandmate. There is Opel, whom Bucky regards as a sort of muse. Bucky notes that her "mind was exceptional" (12), and that she is driven from wealth by a restless desire to experience music and travel. There is also Hanes, the office courier of Bucky's record label, Fenig, the frustrated pulp writer who lives in the apartment above Bucky, and a widow named Micklewhite, who lives downstairs with her cognitively impaired adult son. The son has no name because the parents "never figured he'd live past four months with a head like his head" (134). The novel introduces these characters in its early chapters, which are not divided into "parts" but, rather, are interrupted after the tenth chapter by a "media kit" (including lyrics, press release, and transcripts of interviews) released by Bucky's music management to the press. Several other important characters appear in the ten chapters that follow the "media kit" interchapter: they include Watney, a retired British rock star (and DeLillo's first sketch of the "international" businessman), and Bohack, the leader of the Happy Valley Commune. A second music-industry publication entitled "The Mountain Tapes" follows chapter 20, consisting entirely of lyrics to Bucky's planned release of unreleased songs. And then there is Dr. Pepper, to whose dissembling character I turn below.

Events in *Great Jones Street* follow the sale of "the product," a drug alleged to have been developed by the U.S. government. Its effects are at first unknown but later described as targeting "a particular region in the left hemisphere of the brain, it seems. Where words are kept" (228). The Happy Valley Commune, the group who try to adopt Bucky as a symbol of their ideological return to privacy, have stolen "the product" from a Long Island laboratory and delivered it to Bucky for safekeeping in his apartment on Great Jones Street in the Manhattan neighborhood of Greenwich Village. The commune members wish to sell "the product" to the highest bidder, the news of which precipitates a race to obtain the drug that ultimately involves the majority of the novel's characters. Bucky, who alternates between catatonic disinterest and mild concern, muses on their attempts while considering the path his musical career may take following his departure from the band. Bucky's manager and record company ultimately decide to release Bucky's experimental music, known as "The Mountain Tapes," and his manager Globke plans a tour, telling Bucky: "Don't think of it as a performance. Think of it as an appearance" (198). As it turns out, Hanes, the office courier from the headquarters of Bucky's record company, has used his access to Bucky to strike out on his own and shop "the product." Unbeknownst to Bucky, a series of furtive exchanges and failed sales attempts has taken place, all of which derive from the fact that Hanes had stolen "the product" from Bucky's apartment and traveled to "fifteen cities in three countries" trying to sell it (210). Hanes confesses these facts in the first of the novel's final five chapters. He returns the product and asks Bucky to beg the Happy Valley Commune's pardon for his having stolen the drug.

Enter Dr. Pepper, a narco-pharmacist of legendary stature, who lives underground. Characters in pursuit or possession of "the product" seek Dr. Pepper. They regard him as a prospective buyer or a chemical analyst. The term "character" does not quite apply to Dr. Pepper. Readers first meet him early in the novel, twice, yet neither they nor Bucky know it. When he finally appears as Dr. Pepper more than halfway through the novel, we learn that he also seeks "the product." Styled in the role of an eccentric entrepreneur, he plans to synthesize and mass produce the drug on a global scale, a final pharmacological intervention in mass culture. (He also expresses a desire, common in the novel, to change careers.) In the novel's final chapters, we learn that the person we had earlier thought to be Dr. Pepper may not be Dr. Pepper. In chapter 22, the person speaking as Dr. Pepper offers Bucky an ultimatum: deliver "the product" to him within twenty-four hours, or he will "make arrangements to extend your [Bucky's] sabbatical. You won't leave that room is what I am saying. It will become your past, present and future" (219). In retrospect, the words used in the threat become significant: they describe "the product's" effect.

These varied lines converge in the novel's final two chapters. In the penultimate chapter, Bohack, leader of the Happy Valley Commune, expresses his group's disappointment with Bucky's planned return to music and public life. They have located Hanes and "the product"; in exchange for his life, Hanes, who was upset with Bucky for refusing Hanes's request to return "the product" to Happy Valley, has betrayed the confidence of the record company and revealed the location of the plant where Bucky's new record is being pressed. Bohack offers Bucky the option of suicide and, presumably, a celebrity death that will be romanticized and consumed by his fans and simultaneously preserve the group's desire to maintain Bucky's "privacy" for their own ends. Bucky refuses and follows Bohack to the commune's building. Upon his arrival Bucky is introduced to Fred Chess, who is going to inject "the product" into Bucky. At a certain point Bucky asks, "Are you Dr. Pepper? You're not, are you?" The man replies, "Look, if I were Pepper, it would mean I knew all along what kind of drug was in the package. Any longstanding intimate connection between Happy Valley and Pepper would mean that I, as Pepper, had knowledge of the drug from the very beginning. You'd have to revise everything that's happened. It would mean that I managed not only Bohack but also Hanes and Watney. If I'm Pepper, it means everything's been a lie up to now. . . . It would mean that you've been the victim of the paranoid man's ultimate fear. Everything that is taking place is taking place solely to mislead you. Your reality is managed by others" (253–54).

The truth regarding the mystery of Dr. Pepper's identity is never revealed. Is he Fred Chess, after all? And if so, does that necessitate "revising" one's understanding of the novel's plot? Has Bucky been unwittingly placed in the role of Goethe's Wilhelm Meister, the young man who embarks in *Wilhelm Meister's Apprenticeship* on a journey of self-discovery, only to discover that his travels and encounters have been "managed," to use DeLillo's word, by his elders?

And if Dr. Pepper has orchestrated the plot, then has he also orchestrated Bucky's retreat into privacy? How can one preserve a self or remain "individual" before such deception? Is our privacy a prank we play upon ourselves, a novelist's gimmick to reassure us that we can achieve separation from history? And what if the novelist exposes the artifice of that illusion by turning the conventions of beloved genres against themselves? The possible answers exist simultaneously. They do not offer closure; they defer the responsibility of considering them to the reader, who may wonder, "Have I become a participant in the telling of this story?" In this way *Great Jones Street* replaces the sophisticated yet obtuse narrative scaffolding of DeLillo's prior two novels with more subtle gestures. One hesitates to extend to the reader the "product's" unexpected effects on Bucky, after which Bucky feels that he is "sinking into history" (264), but the effect might be said to anticipate a sort of communion whereby DeLillo's novels begin their long, inward turn, a process that will show its first complete and mature result in the later *White Noise*.

DeLillo's early novels revel in the incongruous possibilities of contemporary American society. Music and business, war and football, cinema and autobiography—they are not paired to offer a panoramic view but to surprise the reader. DeLillo described his choice of subjects to interviewer Anthony DeCurtis: "I've never attempted to embark on a systematic exploration of American experience. I take the ideas as they come."[23] DeLillo's subsequent novels would use other jargons and dialects, other subjects and settings, refining his experiments with language, genre, and narration to different ends; in discussing *Ratner's Star* (1977) in that same interview, he says that "the structure of the book is the book."[24] All the while, the other dramatic elements of his work will also grow in other directions, taking unexpected turns at times and elaborating earlier techniques at others. The later accomplishment might be said to begin with the narrative experiments of these early works, yet reach past them, as if the writer were working even against himself so as to be consistently incongruous with respect to genre and convention.

In the final chapter of *Great Jones Street,* Bucky Wunderlick wanders the streets of lower Manhattan. He is accompanied for a short time by Sandy, the commune member who had brought "the product" to him at the novel's start. Bucky does not speak with her, but his silence has nothing to do with "the product": its effects were temporary, and his brain once again recognizes language. His ability to speak is also restored. He simply chooses not to speak with her. It is unclear whether Sandy still belongs to the Commune or whether the Commune continues to exist at all. She appears ill. Why is Bucky reluctant? Is Sandy shadowing him, a spy monitoring the silence the Commune imposed on him, an enforcer of his involuntary silence? We do not know, we cannot know, but it seems to be the case. If we suspect it, we have become paranoid. Bucky describes the miasmic streets, the proliferation of urban life, with hushed awe. He does not allow anyone to know "the product" failed. Identification with the group or the genre has become suspect to him. Through the reader's proximity to narration, the novel suggests an awkward intimacy: Bucky may be restored to public life, but this is a novel and an individual keeps that secret.

Anthony DeCurtis, a long-standing scholar of DeLillo's fiction, has published one of the few scholarly essays devoted entirely to *Great Jones Street.* DeCurtis admits the book is "not one of DeLillo's more highly regarded novels" and then proceeds to elaborate Bucky's "drawing inward," a process that "would seem to suggest the movement of American society from the political upheavals and turmoil of the late sixties to the dreadful cynicism, deep alienation, and desperate privatism of the seventies."[25] Using quotes from Bob Dylan and Axel Rose as bookends, DeCurtis illustrates how the novel's movement from rock music to "entrepreneurship" illustrates that it is has become increasingly difficult, if not impossible, to find refuge from the joined spheres of publicity and commerce. The problematic anticipates DeLillo's novels of the 1980s, and by the time it has reached its full development in *White Noise* (1985), DeLillo's depiction of the individual's relationship to 1980s consumer culture will result in what is widely considered to be one of the twentieth century's most influential and accomplished novels.

CHAPTER 3

Opacity and Transparency

White Noise and *Mao II*

White Noise

Don DeLillo's eighth novel, *White Noise,* was the first of his books to be issued by the Viking Press, the largest publishing firm with which he had worked until that time. (Viking released the first edition under the imprint of Elizabeth Sifton Books; Sifton had been an editor for the press.) Published in 1985, it was considered by readers to be DeLillo's "breakthrough" work. The novel's publication history and critical reception confirm that status: it was his first novel to receive extensive and nearly unanimous critical praise, the first to be the focus of a collection of scholarly essays (edited by DeLillo scholar Frank Lentricchia and published in 1991), the first to receive a critical edition (edited by DeLillo scholar Mark Osteen and published in 1998), and the first to be reissued in an anniversary edition (published in December 2009, with a new cover design by the illustrator Michael Cho). Viking published all three editions of the novel. To put it simply, in DeLillo's career there is before and after *White Noise.*

Just as DeLillo's career is transformed by the successful publication of *White Noise,* Jack Gladney, the novel's narrator and protagonist, faces a similar "before and after" situation. Jack and his family are exposed together with everyone else in the suburban college town of Blacksmith to the poisonous fumes of a chemical compound named Nyodene Derivative, or Nyodene D. The chemical is released when a tanker car carrying the chemical spills its contents from a nearby railroad line, an event that occurs in the middle of the novel. Fatality does not immediately ensue; rather, Jack learns that the chemical is likely to kill him, that it is already killing him, and that his death will precipitate slowly from "nebulous masses" that are taking form in his body. A causal relationship between the toxin and the masses is never established, however, and there is the possibility that the masses existed prior to the spill. After the fact of contamination and pursuant to medical examination, Jack realizes that Nyodene D resembles everything else (foods, television ads, facts without context, invisible energies emitted by technology) insofar as consumer society thoroughly saturates its participants with the forces—both visible and otherwise—of its influence. In this way the novel implies that it too is immersed in the endless flow of information that permeates every atom of contemporary American life. As such, there is before Nyodene D. and after. Or is there? Like the chemical in question, *White Noise* has an amorphous ability to reshape readers' estimations of all of DeLillo's writings. When considering the writings that precede *White Noise,* readers seem implicitly to ask: "Was DeLillo always this comic, or satirical, or perceptive, or dramatic a writer?" The same is true, perhaps more so (and perhaps unfairly), of the standards to which his later writings are held. Critics often find "trends" in a writer's oeuvre that flatten or disregard certain distinctions. (For instance, look up "DeLillo and Technology," and you will find dozens of publications on the subject.) In any case, the anachronistic "*White Noise*" effect that I describe here is perhaps a common consequence of any outstanding book to which a writer's other achievements are compared. The curious feature of *White Noise* is that the very effect of which I speak in the criticism is built into the novel itself.

In a letter dated January 7, 2001, DeLillo explained the novel's title to its Chinese translator Zhu Ye in the following terms: "The title. There are white noise devices that produce a kind of humming sound in which the intensity is the same at all frequencies. Such a device is designed to protect a person from other distracting or annoying sounds—street noises, aircraft, etc. 'Uniform and white,' as the text says. Jack and other characters associate this phenomenon with the experience of dying. A state in which things are in a perfect balance, perhaps. The title also refers generally to all the unheard (or 'white') noises and other kinds of information routinely engulfing the characters in the book—radio, TV, microwave transmissions, ultrasonic appliances, etc."[1]

DeLillo's letter suggests a different orientation to the materials at hand. The earlier works seem to be structured almost deductively, with characters and dialogue strapped into the novels' obtuse narrative design. In those cases, cinema, genre, or sociolinguistics function as a framework whose details are to be inserted after the fact. *White Noise* opens a new trajectory with respect to the narrative structure of DeLillo's works: the narrative scaffolding does not so much vanish as it is internalized by the characters. After all, how can one dramatize "frequencies" and "sounds" and "nebulous masses"? How does one depict the synesthesia of a "noise" being "white?" A poet might answer these questions in verse. A novelist must dramatize events in the form of a plot along which the development of ideas takes narrative form in description, dialogue, and affect. What if the plot itself were to internalize its materials, develop the ominous notion, present from the novel's first words, that all objects were in some way connected into a single field of relations for which "white noise" functions as the figural phrasing? A field of relations that has also the uncanny capacity to enter and reconfigure the reader's thoughts? What if the commodity form of the novel were a way of internalizing those very notions in the reader's mind—a sort of literary contamination, as it were?

The novel begins with a description of parents delivering students to school at the beginning of the college year. The prose is dominated by nouns; lists of commodities, accumulating by way of the passive voice, initially crowd out the actors: "The roofs of the station wagons were loaded down with carefully secured suitcases full of light and heavy clothing; with boxes of blankets, boots and shoes, stationery and books, sheets, pillows, quilts; with rolled-up rucksacks and sleeping bags" (3). Jack Gladney reveals himself to be the narrator after he suspends his viewing of this avalanche of student amenities. The viewing never truly ends; as we shall see, one of the novel's distinguishing narrative features is its subterranean style of discourse: its conversations, meditations, and descriptions never break off. They travel instead along inaccessible channels only to resurface suddenly at some later point. Like Jack, *White Noise* internalizes things as if it too were alive.

Such a complicated and clever style of narration poses obvious challenges to the reader as well as the reviewer and critic. They are welcome challenges, of course, in that they result from the novel's formidably amorphous narrative design. Jack Gladney and the family of which he is a part constitute its most tangible dramatic elements. Their presentation in the novel provides contrast to DeLillo's earlier writings; the family itself embodies the dispersed, numinous qualities of the novel's title; and critics of the novel have much to say about the family and its individual characters. As such, the family offers an obvious starting point for discussion, as it is the filter through which Jack's narration is largely refined.

The Gladney family brings family melodrama to mind. In many ways *White Noise* was the first major work of American literary postmodernism to consider a family as central to its design in some way. For decades American novelists had more often than not denied genealogy (see the opening lines of Salinger's *Catcher in the Rye*), or illustrated how historical forces had broken families apart (Morrison's *The Bluest Eye,* Doctorow's *The Book of Daniel*), or portrayed characters escaping from families (Pynchon's *The Crying of Lot 49*). Domesticity, if it appeared in any way, was fraught with terror and shame, or it was a homebound biographical premise from which to flee into America. (DeLillo's *Americana* entertains the latter notion, if only to complicate it.) In addition, the damaging consequence of a family's absence was also the subject of great novels (see, for example, Joan Didion's *Play It As It Lays*). Considered in relation to the institution of the American novel, the families in the majority of postmodern literary narratives clashed against or drifted away from the great genealogical lines that ran through the writings of Faulkner and Steinbeck. Restoration of a mythical American family is not, however, the goal of *White Noise.* DeLillo's previous novels offered only glimpses of families. In those moments, the family was either a memory (David's in *Americana* is the most extensive) or a domestic premise to be displaced, for the sake of contrast, by a larger plot (Lyle and Pammy's marriage in DeLillo's 1977 novel *Players*). Until *White Noise* DeLillo's characters had inhabited the postgenealogical culture of Holden Caulfield rather than the patrilineal (and later matrilineal) culture of Tom Joad.

The Gladneys of *White Noise* are in effect a composite made from parts of several different marriages. Their genealogies are fragile and difficult to trace across the book. The character playing the role of husband is Jack, and the one playing the role of wife is Babette. Husband and wife are not synonymous with the biological roles of mother and father vis-à-vis every child who lives with them, of whom there are four. Wilder, the youngest, is Babette's son by birth. Wilder's father is an anonymous man who lives in the Australian outback with a second, older son named Eugene. Steffie, the second youngest child, is Jack's daughter from his second marriage to a woman named Dana Breedlove. Wilder and Steffie are followed in age by two teenagers. Denise, who is eleven years old, is Babette's child from her first husband, Jack Pardee (a hustler of sorts who makes a brief visit to the home). Heinrich, the oldest, is Jack's son from his second marriage to his first wife, Janet Savory, who "has taken the name Mother Devi" and who lives and works in an ashram "located on the outskirts of the former copper-smelting town of Tubb, Montana, now called Dharamsalapur" (24). In addition to the aforementioned Eugene, who is Babette's son (and Wilder's older brother), there are two other siblings living afar: Heinrich's sister lives with his mother, and Jack also has a second daughter, Bee, from his third wife, Tweedy Browner. In total, Jack has been married five times to four women and Babette has been married three times to three men. Combined, they have seven children, four of whom live in Blacksmith with Jack and Babette.

In a very useful article that he published during the first wave of scholarly writings about *White Noise,* Thomas Ferraro noted the following about this family structure: "Not a single child whom Babette has mothered or whom Jack has fathered, whether in their custody or not, is living with both parents or even a full brother or sister. Above all, the current assemblage has not been together longer than Wilder's two years of age, and in all probability less than that."[2] Ferraro proceeds to show how DeLillo's novel does not align with the social theories of intellectuals such as Christopher Lasch or Allan Bloom, figures who scowled in their respective ways about the dissolution of the American family. (In an important section of the article, Ferraro illustrates how consumerism replaces biological bonds so as to sustain the Gladney kinship.)

Similar patterns of relations shape the criticism of the novel. Ferraro's article appeared in a 1991 volume entitled *New Essays on* White Noise, edited by Ferraro's Duke University colleague Frank Lentrichhia, who in that same year edited a collection of essays entitled *Introducing Don DeLillo.* Although the two books were released in the same year, the "new" in the former volume's title refers to the fact that the latter volume contained writings on *White Noise* and that most of that volume's essays had already been printed in 1990 in a special issue of the journal *South Atlantic Quarterly.* In those volumes, critics such as Anthony DeCurtis, John McClure, Lentricchia, Daniel Aaron, and others would shape much of the criticism devoted to DeLillo's writings. As we saw in the previous chapter, McClure devoted early writings to DeLillo's use of genre in his novels. (In the present case, Ferraro devotes attention to sociological matters such as the family and the role of technology in society.) Some of those critics continued to write about DeLillo over the decades that followed, while others departed to other critical formations. For instance, DeCurtis and McClure continued to publish important writings about DeLillo, and it should be noted that McClure was the first to write on the question of the secular in DeLillo's writings. They were joined by other figures in DeLillo criticism such as Mark Osteen, Tom LeClair, and John N. Duvall, and many of them followed DeLillo's career and continue writing about it to the present day. As the Gladneys gather in ad hoc familial relations around consumption, intellectuals also gravitate in comparable formations to the object of their scientific study. One might call it coincidental mimesis.

Experts from other areas of literary scholarship have also contributed to the understanding of DeLillo's writings. (Linda S. Kauffman's fine recent essays on *Falling Man* are an excellent example of the habit.) Their contributions have come in many valuable forms. Leonard Orr, a renowned scholar of modern literatures, offered one such contribution in a concise 2003 volume entitled *Don DeLillo's* White Noise, remarking upon the novel's presentation of the Gladney family. He writes that "information about the dispersed Gladney family . . . is not given in any one long passage of exposition, but is spread throughout the novel, so the first appearance makes the family seem more solid and home-centered than it is."[3] Returning to my earlier comment regarding the novel's narrative structure, we might consider the Gladney family structure a microcosm, or better still a microclimate, within the novel. The family absorbs and metabolizes information from the larger atmosphere. (In Jack's case, it also metastasizes.) As it does so, it generates facts about itself in the manner in which the media transmits news of the toxic event: in a form that is "dispersed," to borrow Orr's term, like the toxic cloud.

The novel's dispersion of genealogical information serves another function that is central to the debates surrounding *White Noise:* the question of characterization. *The Body Artist* (2001), a book that is arguably the most attentive to the development of character among those DeLillo has published to date, adopts a similar narrative technique. The narration of that book's first scene weaves description of birds that fly about the yard outside the kitchen window. There is no parody about nature there, no cue that would make the reader think for a single moment that the fragmented descriptive passages are meant to focus on anything but the sober and poignant scene unfolding in the room. There too the description is "dispersed" over the course of the text. I discuss that scene in the following chapter but would apply its logic here so as to compare it with the narrative structure of *White Noise,* which is organized in a similar manner with respect to the Gladney family, and with considerable consequence for individual characters.

Characterization and affect have divided critical opinion of DeLillo's writing more than any other question. The point of debate is this: how does one evaluate characters that are claimed not to resemble "real" people in that they lack the capacity to convey feeling? Take, for instance, chapter 7 of *White Noise.* It is divided by two distinct moods. In the first, Jack and Babette are in their bedroom, where they discuss the prospect of sex in the most absurd, comic fashion imaginable, exchanging seriocomic banter that displaces the erotic premise. Despite its banality (or perhaps because of it), Jack becomes sexually aroused. The couple resolves to read an erotic publication; Jack offers a brief discourse on irony, noting that it is "the means by which we rescue ourselves from the past" (30). He leaves the room to obtain "a trashy magazine" but returns with a family photo album. The emotional momentum of the narration turns on a dime, and the chapter closes with a poignant rumination in which the family looks through the scrapbooks and photographs. In the chapter's paratactic final sentence, the narration poses a question that has been creeping into Jack's mind in earlier chapters, and it resurfaces here as if it had suddenly entered the room to join the reminiscing family: "Who will die first?" In this chapter, two moods are juxtaposed to a dramatic affective result, and then a final line of narration that had temporarily submerged suddenly reappears.

It is not the only passage or even chapter of this kind in the novel. Babette asserts her autonomy in a later chapter when she reveals her infidelity to Jack, and there too the mood shifts from comedic delirium to somber reflection. The same might be said for the scene when the Gladneys return from a shopping spree and each one of them wishes "to be left alone" (84). My point is that it is difficult, even impossible, to reduce the Gladneys to a one-dimensional parody of the American family. I admit the anachronism, in that I have used DeLillo's later novel as evidence. But when looking back upon his earlier writings with the more recent fiction in mind, we see the clear precedent: the sincerity of the passage derives from the "dispersed" narrative organization. One effect is to provide proof of DeLillo's ability to write substantial dramatic characters with and through an inventive telling of the plot; another is that the narration requires that readers recalibrate their understanding of character so as to recognize an integral relation between characterization and narrative design. In a novel such as this one, which is very much committed to depicting how mass media inflects characterization, it is useful to remember Marshall McLuhan's slogan "The medium is the message." This is not to say that the novel's characters are indistinct or simple media effects; rather, distinguishing elements of character—such as emotion—are also "dispersed" over the narration, and inseparable from it.

Many of DeLillo's reviewers of this period nonetheless assailed his characters for their lack of "substance." The charges against DeLillo came from various quarters. Fellow novelists such as John Updike pilloried his style (Updike once early in DeLillo's career and then again a quarter century later). DeLillo has also been taken to task by intellectuals of the academy who regard him as a representative of an obsolete brand of disaffected postmodernism. Bitter invective came also from conservative intellectual journalists. In a 1985 review-essay originally published in the *New Criterion*, literary critic Bruce Bawer wrote: "There should be profound emotions at work here, but *White Noise* is, like its predecessors, so masterfully contrived a piece of argumentation that believable human actions and feelings are few and far between."[4] Bawer proceeded to note that for DeLillo "life seems to exist so that we can theorize about it." Bawer considers *White Noise* an essay masquerading as a novel, littered with bits of "rapidly aging nihilistic clichés" about contemporary American life.[5] Curiously, Bawer's argument resembles similar claims about DeLillo's characters posed by critics from the academic left (yet without the resentment regarding DeLillo's alleged bleak vision of America). In a later review, the influential conservative columnist George F. Will adopted a line of argument similar to Bower's when he reviewed DeLillo's 1988 novel *Libra*. Will described DeLillo's writing as "an act of literary vandalism and bad citizenship" insofar as "DeLillo's attempt to 'follow the bullets' trajectories' back into the minds of Lee Harvey Oswald and others becomes yet another exercise in blaming America for Oswald's act of derangement."[6]

Scholars and champions of DeLillo's writing have responded to such negative evaluations in a number of different ways. Eugene Goodheart appealed to precedent to justify DeLillo's characters. In "Don DeLillo and the Cinematic Real," Goodheart argued that "the deliberate insubstantiality of DeLillo's characters is compensated for by an extraordinary and eloquent plenitude of speech."[7] Goodheart alludes here to DeLillo's oft-stated admission that characterization, or the criticism of his characterizations, does not bother him.[8] In explaining dialogue, scholars have also deferred to artistic influence when explaining the discursive inclinations of DeLillo's characters, as Mark Osteen has done in noting the influence of Jean-Luc Godard's cinematic "essays" on DeLillo's fiction (an influence that DeLillo readily admits).[9]

Describing his writing of characters, and indirectly justifying Goodheart's claim, DeLillo noted in a later interview that "I want to give pleasure through language, through the architecture of a book or sentence and through characters who may be funny, nasty, violent, or all of these. But I'm not the kind of writer who dotes on certain characters to the degree that he's able to work out their existence."[10] In addition, reviewers might have noted that DeLillo varies the depth of characterization from novel to novel: "I think about dialogue differently from book to book. In *The Names* I raised the level of intelligence and perception. In *Libra* I flattened things out. The characters are bigger and broader, the dialogue is flatter."[11]

Justifications such as these are very useful, but they also unnecessarily concede ground to critics who, for the most part, had not bothered to study DeLillo very carefully before attacking his work. (In accusing DeLillo of pandering to conspiracy and paranoia about the Kennedy assassination, George F. Will conveniently ignored an interview, published in *Vogue* several weeks prior to Will's review, in which DeLillo stated that "to my knowledge, there was no specific cover-up [in the Warren Commission Report].")[12]

Frank Lentricchia's essay "The American Writer as Bad Citizen" provides a memorable and devastating exception. In that essay, Lentricchia argued on the one hand against literary critics who, in dismissing DeLillo's novels, implicitly advocate the "the comforts of our [American] stability [that] require a minor, apolitical domestic fiction of the triumphs and agonies of autonomous private individuals."[13] In this line of argument, according to Lentricchia, DeLillo's ambitions are regarded as "pretentious in the setting of the new regionalism," the latter being a homespun, semiautobiographical fiction.[14] Lentricchia concludes that "unlike these new regionalists of and for the Reagan eighties, DeLillo (or Joan Didion, or Toni Morrison, or Cynthia Ozick, or Norman Mailer) offers us no myth of political virginity preserved, no 'individuals' who are not expressions of—and responses to—specific historical processes."[15] In Lentricchia's view, terms such as "provincialism" and "regionalism" are synonymous with the conservatism of artists and intellectuals inhabiting the left wing of the critical spectrum.

Lentricchia proceeds to address the conservatism exemplified by Bawer and Will. He begins by noting that DeLillo's recent success (beginning with the award he received in 1984 from the American Academy and Institute of Arts and Letters, and through the publication of *White Noise* and *Libra*) indicates "the best sign of [DeLillo's] cultural relevance in our day: the media political right has begun to take an active interest in DeLillo."[16] Lentricchia then responds primarily to Will's attack against *Libra.* (He also cites Bawer's criticism of *White Noise* in its appeal to implicit American virtues, though, admittedly, Bawer's view is more literary and lacks the virulent, ad hominem insults that characterize Will's invective.) Lentricchia notes a common thread among the reviewers: that they cannot explain DeLillo without appealing to a false notion that fiction must be solely populated by characters who conform to common-sense notions of literary realism or, more precisely, a distorted notion of literary realism. Having exposed the false literary assumptions and criteria of their arguments, Lentricchia furthermore concludes that "the media right has nevertheless said, in so many words . . . that fiction does not have a private address and that DeLillo does to Oswald what we, for good or ill, do every day to our friends, lovers, and enemies: he interprets him, he creates a character."[17]

Lentricchia's polemic is as relevant today as when it was written twenty years ago. In addition, he defends DeLillo's characterizations. Nevertheless, both DeLillo's detractors and defenders lose sight of a rather important fact along the way: that DeLillo's characters are harnessed to the narration of his novels. To some degree, it is simply impossible to defend or attack DeLillo's fiction on ideological grounds or on the grounds of "realism" without first addressing *how* the novelist assembles words on the page. This is not to make the case for an abstract and empty formalism or the type of analysis that would reduce DeLillo's novels to something resembling architectural blueprints. Rather, I would take the long view and argue that the essayistic discursions offered by characters in DeLillo's novels (a habit to which both Bawer and Will forcefully object, and which Goodheart and Osteen defend) are the dramatic surface effects of an artful series of narrative experiments that can be traced over the course of DeLillo's career. Beginning with the faux–Jean-Luc Godard narrative/cinematic experiments of *Americana* and continuing through his experiments with genre during the 1970s, DeLillo's fiction develops a centripetal narrative motion to match the centrifugal and wide-ranging subjects of his novels, or what Lentricchia calls in writers like DeLillo "an effort to represent their culture in its totality."[18]

White Noise marks a turning point in this arc of narrative development because while on its surface it appears to experiment with genre and its broad cultural framework, the novel's primary orientation is introspective. As I noted, the novel contains the base elements of a family melodrama. As with his second novel, *End Zone, White Noise* also doubles as a campus novel. Jack Gladney is chair of the Department of Hitler Studies at College on the Hill. During the course of a lecture (he teaches one class, once a week), Jack delivers a monologue that was for many years a touchstone for DeLillo's critics. Jack describes the scene and recounts the speech: "When the showing ended, someone asked about the plot to kill Hitler. The discussion moved to plots in general. I found myself saying to the assembled heads: 'All plots tend to move deathward. This is the nature of plots. Political plots, terrorist plots, lovers' plots, narrative plots, plots that are part of children's games. We edge near death every time we plot. It is like a contract that all must sign, the plotters as well as those who are targets of the plot'" (26). The sentence fragment that begins with "Political plots" typifies a type of construction well-known to DeLillo's readers: the "list."

DeLillo includes such lists in the majority of his writings. They often appear as sequences of nouns; we find them, for example, in *Americana* when Sullivan says, "neon, fiberglass, plexiglass" (127) to David. They also take lyrical form as the sing-song babble of Bucky's song lyrics in *Great Jones Street* or as the ritualized pregame exercises of the football team in *End Zone,* described by the narrator as "frantic breathing with elements of chant" (106). In these earlier instances the chanting or repetition of lists often functions as an accent to stress a relevant point: the football players' chants reinforce Gary's faux-anthropological view of the locker room. In *White Noise* the lists serve to blur the line between character and milieu (whereas in the case of *End Zone,* the lists create a narrative distance). The first such list appears in chapter 10 of *White Noise.* The narration cuts abruptly from Jack's conversation with his colleague Murray Siskind to Jack and Babette walking through town. There is no indication of who is speaking, as pronouns render the actors opaque. Jack asks Babette about her recent amnesia as they pass an optics store. The words "Dacron, Orlon, Lycra Spandex" (52) interrupt the narration. They are the names of synthetic textiles, but they are not spoken as dialogue. They might be words that Jack or Babette sees in advertisements as they pass windows, or associations that one of the characters' makes after passing a clothing store.

In a later scene, Jack watches his daughter Steffie as she sleeps on a cot in the evacuation center where the Gladneys seek refuge from the toxic cloud. Jack hears her mumble something in her sleep. He waits, then hears, "*Toyota Celica.*" Jack reflects upon the "near-nonsense words," describing them as "supranational names, computer-generated, more or less universally pronounceable. Part of every child's brain noise, the substatic regions too deep to probe. Whatever its source, the utterance struck me with the impact of a moment of splendid transcendence" (155). The last effect may be induced by the chemicals in the air (an effect comparable to the citizens' newfound sensitivity to the post-spill sunsets), but the narrative voicing must also be noted. DeLillo had already used scrolling lists of commodities to set the stage in the novel's first paragraph. In all three scenes mentioned above—the "plot" speech, the conversation, and this one—the mantra-like lists erupt from the narration without warning or a specific cause. DeLillo had already set the stage in the opening novel's first paragraph, as the lists of commodities scroll by without any hint that we see them from Jack's point of view. In all three of the scenes mentioned above—the "plot" speech, the conversation, and this one—the mantra-like lists appear without warning or any clear causation. Even if we can attribute them to the context of a character's action, as in the case of Jack's speech, the grammatical constructions themselves often seem like media sound bites that DeLillo has inserted into the dialogue. Over time, the chanted noun-lists become an elemental, linguistic analog to the multiform "white noise" of a consumer society that blurs distinctions between inanimate objects and sentient ones. Certain characters in the novel, such as Murray, seem to be already aware of the phenomenon, while others respond to it by seeking refuge from it or lashing out against it with violence. Confused and terrorized by its mystery, Babette turns to experimental drug treatments, while Jack lashes out against Mr. Gray, the man who provides the drugs (which ultimately fail) to Babette. Their conjoined responses only make matters worse. In the end Jack returns to the passive state of the novel's opening paragraph, as the final paragraph begins, "The supermarket shelves have been arranged," and the descriptions of things accumulate to the novel's famous closing fragments: "The tales of the supernatural and the extraterrestrial. The miracle vitamins, the cures for cancer, the remedies for obesity. The cults of the famous and the dead" (326).

DeLillo's expert readers have generally focused on the implication rather than the means of the novel's fusion of objects with characters. As we have seen, his champions regard *White Noise* as an elevated form of cultural criticism, and his opponents treat it as an impoverished or even immoral one. These are largely ideological positions (what is not?), yet the fact of the matter is that they also put the cart before the proverbial horse by primarily treating the novel as a political tract rather than as an object of art. When regarded in the latter view, one would be honest to admit that Ralph Ellison's *Invisible Man*—one of the most celebrated political novels in modern human history—is likely the only American novel of the Cold War to fuse narrator with narration to greater effect.

As noted earlier, *White Noise* attracted a host of commentators to DeLillo's writings for the first time. Many have offered explanations of various aspects of the work, and some commentators focus on the chants, mantras, and lists that recur throughout DeLillo's fiction. One of the first to do so was Daniel Aaron, who commented at length on the speech of DeLillo's characters (and in its defense). Aaron's experimental essay mixes commentary with quotation; he imitates DeLillo's style, using sentence fragments to add emphasis to his comments on DeLillo's style. (Aaron had clearly read all of DeLillo's novels.) Aaron devotes a long section of the essay to the "concise observations [often in the form of aphorisms]" made by DeLillo's characters and how those observations "can often lengthen into little essays."[19] Aaron discusses the "crazies," obsessives, narrators, and novelists who are "quick," in Aaron's view, "[to] spot the extraordinary in the commonplace" because they are "sensitive to shades and nuances, sounds and colors and . . . they read the language of movements and gestures."[20] At one point, Aaron uses the example of Dr. Pepper in *Great Jones Street* to introduce the question of "glossolalia," or speaking in tongues. Together with repetitive chanting and aphasia, or speechlessness, glossolalia is a common subject of commentary on DeLillo's fiction.

In interviews DeLillo has often described his interest in linguistic forms of liminal or spiritual experience, a category that includes glossolalia, aphasia, and chant. In a 1982 interview, he defined it as a concern with the "'untellable' points to the limitations of language," elements that include childlike "babbling" (exemplified by Wilder's communication in *White Noise*) and glossolalia that suggests "there's another way to speak . . . a different language lurking somewhere in the brain."[21] DeLillo returned to the subject of chanting in a 1993 interview, where he discusses the scene in which Steffie repeats a brand name in her sleep: "There's something nearly mystical about certain words and phrases that float through our lives. . . . When you detach one of these words from the product it was designed to serve, the word acquires a chantlike quality. . . . If you concentrate on the sound, if you dissociate the words from the object they denote, and if you say the words over and over, they become a kind of higher Esperanto. This is how *Toyota Celica* began its life. It was pure chant at the beginning."[22]

Nearly every major critical study of DeLillo's writings published during the past quarter century has addressed the matter of language in DeLillo's prose, and often with emphasis on the alternate counterlanguages described above. In his book *American Magic and Dread* (2000), Mark Osteen discusses glossolalia as a form of revelatory spiritual experience (in his example, that of Pentecostal Christianity). Summarizing DeLillo scholar Tom LeClair's earlier writings on the subject, Osteen argues that DeLillo's novels expose readers to heteroglossia, by which "we cannot read words as obsessive trackers of univocal meaning" and begin to perceive them instead as "the marriage of oppositions, including that of orality and literacy."[23] In a more recent discussion of glossolalia in DeLillo's fiction, Peter Boxall notes that heteroglossia takes a punitive form in DeLillo's *Underworld* (1997). In his view, the global ascent of consumerism and the universalist aspirations of its linguistic shorthand (the "higher Esperanto," as DeLillo called it) result in exclusion rather than revelation. Aligning the novel with precedents in Milton and Hawthorne, Boxall argues that "the entire narrative wheels away from that opening half-line, discovering, despite itself, all those forms of cultural experience and memory that cannot be articulated by an American voice, that remain unknown, untranslatable, unnameable."[24] Glossolalia becomes in this view a rather secular matter: it is the linguistic waste of an empire.

An even more recent essay, published by renowned DeLillo scholar David Cowart, includes discussion of the character of Mr. Tuttle in DeLillo's *The Body Artist* (2001), a character who mimics the speech of others. Other critics have begun to consider DeLillo's rendering of language and Alzheimer's disease in *Falling Man* (2007), and in more general terms, critical writings on DeLillo's recent fiction have consistently offered compelling and thoughtful discussions of the inventive, idiosyncratic, and quasi-mystical languages that appear in his fiction. Cowart summarizes the matter nicely in the opening lines of his essay when he writes, "One cannot, in any event, overemphasize the centrality of the language theme in any and all of DeLillo's novels, stories, plays and essays."[25]

As such, the discussion of dialogue, language, linguistic divergence, liminality, and even silence (Bucky Wunderlick's feigned aphasia) informs much of the critical writing that celebrates DeLillo's contributions to the American novel. Nearly all the major schools of poststructuralist literary studies (chief among them deconstruction and semiotics) have engaged its role in his fiction; those critical modes inclined to the social sciences (chief among them ethnic studies and women's studies) have commented upon it; and scholars from film studies and cultural studies, as well as performance studies, disability studies, and eco-criticism, have contributed to a diverse and vibrant discussion of DeLillo's literary language.

Language is by no means the only interesting focus of discussion in the long dialogues that have shaped understanding of DeLillo's fiction. Its high standing in the study of DeLillo's work results in part from the fact that it is the duty of literary critics to regard language as the primary material of literary artistic labor. It is also the necessary consequence of reading the novels, not only to generate professional criticism but simply because DeLillo's novels offer an elevated and extraordinarily refined view of American English and its variants. I have regarded the aesthetic role that DeLillo affords to nouns vis-à-vis narration and characterization in *White Noise*. In this view, that novel represents a turn away from his earlier techniques but also an extension of them into new moods and modes. I have also stressed the matter so as to emphasize that while "language" remains a constant emphasis in his work, the means of its delivery changes. If it were a form of state-sponsored political propaganda, one might say the "deep state" that delivers *White Noise* had come to power through a coup d'état that displaced a previous narrative regime in his fiction.

Never one to avoid shocking his audience, however, DeLillo crafted his novel *Mao II* (1991) so as to portray a novelist whose language and trade are besieged by a new form of discourse that speaks in images rather than words. The result is an explicitly political work of literary fiction that ventured even to experiment with mixed media, as it integrated photographs and paintings into its narrative design.

Mao II

Twenty years had passed since the Houghton Mifflin Company of Boston published Don DeLillo's first novel, *Americana,* in 1971. DeLillo changed publishers for his fourth novel, *Ratner's Star* (1976), moving to Alfred A. Knopf, the famed New York publishing firm. With *White Noise* he switched again to the prestigious Viking Press, which in the mid-1970s had become a subsidiary of the Penguin Publishing Group, the world's largest publisher of literary fiction. Viking made *White Noise* a success, and the novel's successor, *Libra,* became DeLillo's first best-seller. Copies of DeLillo's subsequent novels were printed by the hundreds of thousands.

The curious reader who stumbled upon a rare copy of DeLillo's first novel in chapter 2, and who perhaps followed DeLillo's career, would no longer have to seek out stray copies. This was partly because of DeLillo's success, but it was also because of how the business of book publishing had changed during those twenty years. DeLillo made that change a central concern of his ninth novel, *Mao II* (1991). The novel's first chapter depicts a character named Scott, the younger personal assistant to the reclusive novelist Bill Gray, in a large New York City bookstore. Scott walks through the store from one level to another scrutinizing the commerce of books. He notes their significant placement in the store, how they are "stacked on tables and set in clusters near the cash terminals," how the stacks are "arranged in artful fanning patterns" and "step terraces and Lucite wall-shelves" (19). Distinctions are made between hardcover books, with Scott "fitting hand over sleek spine, seeing lines of type jitter past his thumb," and paperbacks, whose "covers were lacquered and gilded." The scene describes the heyday of the large retail bookseller, that class of national bookstores that adopted the franchise model of corporate development during the 1970s and thereby dominated the retail book business.

Book-selling and the business of literary publishing vex Bill Gray throughout the novel. Indeed the novel's premise is that Bill progressively rejects them. The novel proceeds in later chapters to describe Bill's working habits, Scott's management of his papers, Bill's aversion to publicity and biography, and the harrowing expectations of an unpredictable audience. In the middle of a conversation regarding the novel's central political conflict, Bill interrupts his editor to ask, "Remember literature, Charlie? It involved being drunk and getting laid" (122).

The political conflict in question resembles in many ways what came to be known as the "Rushdie Affair," a story in which DeLillo's publisher played an important role. In the fall of 1988, Viking-Penguin published Salman Rushdie's *The Satanic Verses* in England. Literary critics largely praised the book, but Indian Muslims (Rushdie was born one)—journalists, clerics, and politicians—objected to characters and events that seemed to allude to the Prophet Mohammed.[26] British Muslims responded in outrage to the news, burning copies of Rushdie's books and organizing mass protests. Protestors demanded the book be banned and withdrawn and that Rushdie be prosecuted for blasphemy. British booksellers were bombed. In February 1989, the Iranian cleric Ayatollah Khomeini pronounced a death sentence against Rushdie that included a multimillion-dollar reward to the Iranian who might kill the writer (the reward being one million dollars for a non-Iranian). Salman Rushdie and his wife, novelist Marianne Wiggins, were quickly placed under the protection of the British Secret Services and forced into hiding. British journalist William J. Weatherby consulted Columbia University literary scholar and Palestinian exile Edward W. Said while writing the first book on the Rushdie Affair. In that book Weatherby quotes Said as saying that Rushdie "didn't anticipate what Kohmeini would do."[27]

While Rushdie was the primary target, protestors also targeted booksellers, publishers, and translators. Under siege by constant bomb threats, the headquarters of Viking-Penguin was forced in several countries to hire security for its staff. American writers found themselves faced with a choice: to defend Rushdie and the principle of freedom of artistic expression, to criticize him (as some British authors had done), or to avoid controversy. The *New York Times* published writers in support of Rushdie. They included Chinua Achebe, Nadine Gordimer, Elie Wiesel, and Ralph Ellison. In addition to Ellison, other American authors, including Susan Sontag, Norman Mailer, Thomas Pynchon, James Michener, and Stephen King, defended Rushdie. Yet publishers and booksellers continued to fret over the American edition of Rushdie's novel. They had good reason to do so. As Weatherby notes, "Early in March, too, the office of the *Riverdale Press,* a New York City weekly newspaper, was fire bombed and all but destroyed" because the paper had published an editorial defending "the right to publish, to distribute and to sell *The Satanic Verses.*"[28]

DeLillo's novels had always engaged contemporary events with inventive, indirect artfulness. They often represented the great countercultural themes of the era: Vietnam (*Americana, End Zone, Running Dog*), psychedelia (*Great Jones Street*), and conspiracy culture (*Players, The Names, White Noise,* and *Libra*). DeLillo has also attuned fiction to the intersection where terrorism converged with capital (in *Players,* as well as in the later *Cosmopolis*). *Mao II* is certainly among those books, and much of it confirms that DeLillo followed the Rushdie Affair with interest and concern. The novel's language even escaped into his other statements and writings of that period. Philip Nel described it as follows: "In a 1991 interview, DeLillo repeated one of [Bill] Grey's speeches without acknowledging he was doing so. *The Rushdie Defense Pamphlet,* which DeLillo co-wrote with Paul Auster, borrows a phrase from Gray when it says 'the principle of free expression, the democratic shout, is far less audible than it was five years ago.'"[29] And so the reader who follows Scott into the large bookstore portrayed in *Mao II* to purchase a copy of the novel is faced with an immediate question: does one read the novel as an allegory of the Rushdie Affair?

It is useful to step back and take the long view so as to approach the matter from a different angle. Certain novels can fairly be said to define a writer's legacy. More precisely, teachers, critics, students, curators, and varied audiences of readers, as well as other artists, succeed in persuading generations of readers to regard certain literary works as "definitive." A writer is thus defined in relation to a single work, the obstinacy of which pervades our literary memory. Associate a novel with the following names: Fitzgerald. Hawthorne. Kerouac. Hurston. Melville. Steinbeck. Lists of this sort can suggest associations as well as obscure them. They become hypnotic.

White Noise is often considered the "breakthrough" work of DeLillo's literary career. It is admittedly very much unlike the novels that preceded it. DeLillo has himself noted the difference but without specifying a particular novel. Generally speaking, he regards his novels of the 1980s—*The Names, White Noise,* and *Libra*—as marking a shift in his work. Each of those novels was more distinct with respect to its predecessors, and one might date a slightly different cluster—*White Noise, Libra,* and *Mao II*—as definitive in a collective rather than individual sense. *White Noise* closes the door on the narrative experiments with genre in the first period of DeLillo's career as a novelist, but it also opens another door onto the more introspective, character-driven fiction of the period that follows. While sharing many of the traits of this later period, *Mao II* is also a different animal, a sort of wild card to remind readers that DeLillo's career has been as unpredictable as it has been consistent.

Mao II has two main parts, each consisting of several chapters. DeLillo included two additional parts that function as kinds of bookends to the novel. The first, entitled "At Yankee Stadium," focuses primarily on the point of view of Karen Janney, a young American woman who is at that moment a bride in the mass wedding ritual described in that part of the book; the second bookend, entitled "In Beirut," focuses on Brita Nillson, a Scandinavian photographer working on assignment during the civil war in Lebanon. DeLillo populates the novel with an ensemble cast. It includes primarily Bill, Brita, Scott, and Karen, but also Charlie, Bill's editor, George Haddad, a spokesman for a group of militant Lebanese Maoists, and Jean-Claude Julien, an unknown Swiss poet who has been kidnapped by the aforementioned terrorists. Karen begins the novel and Brita ends it, and their stories are intertwined with others so that the reader can never lose sight of the fact that the narration favors their points of view. Maria Nadotti interviewed DeLillo in 1993, and her questions turned to the women characters in *Mao II.* Nadotti asked, "Has Brita, who is hired to photograph Bill Gray in *Mao II,* perhaps found a way to escape invisibility by reversing the terms and becoming herself a perceiving subject rather than a perceived object?" And DeLillo responded to her, "Reversing the terms? In a sense, yes. She is in this way exercising a certain control over people. In the case of the book, moreover, she is photographing a man."[30]

DeLillo has always taken a sophisticated view of the dynamics of perception, and while his recent novels had become more "literary," *Mao II* is, as some have called it, a work of "mixed media" insofar as the book itself integrates the very images to which it refers. In the first place, the novel offers a running commentary on the paintings that adorn its original dust jacket: Andy Warhol's *Mao* series (1972–74). The title page of each of *Mao II*'s four parts features a photograph. In the first case, the reader sees a reproduction of a black and white photograph of a mass wedding. The brides and grooms file past a religious figure. In the second image, which precedes part 1, a crowd of spectators at a sporting event are crushed against a fence, their faces distorted, panicked, or lifeless. In the third photograph, which precedes part 2, a crowd is gathered beneath a massive photograph from which the Iranian cleric Ayatollah Khomeini scowls back at the viewer; the photo depicts the scene at the Ayatollah's funeral. Finally, there is a photograph of three boys crouching in what appear to be the cement ruins of a building. One of them is raising two fingers in a "V" sign and smiling at his hand, one stares out of the frame, and the third returns the viewer's gaze through what appears to be a viewfinder. In the novel Brita and Karen actually view these images or participate in the scenes they depict: Karen watches the riots at the soccer game and funeral on television and also takes part in the wedding; Brita is present in Beirut.

Karen and Brita have differing relations to visual media. Brita is a participant who creates it, where Karen is defined more by her perception and consumption of it. Throughout the novel, Karen plays the role of participant-observer. Laura Barrett perfectly described that role in a recent essay on the novel's mixed-media design when she noted, "Shading into the image, Karen simultaneously observes the scene and participates in it."[31] Synesthesia is the bridge over which Karen crosses to the streets of lower Manhattan, looking for Bill, in part 2 of the novel. The sounds and smells heighten her sensitivity to color and light, triggering an effect comparable to what Warhol had achieved in coloring the portrait of Chairman Mao. She spends her days among the homeless denizens of a public park, following a teenager named Omar as he sells and delivers narcotics. At night she watches broadcasts of Chinese troops and Iranian mourners on a television at Brita's apartment. She reverts to her former spiritualism (she had been a follower of the Reverend Sun Myung Moon, whom she calls "Master," and her deprogramming from the cult was not complete) and wanders the park, speaking in broken English as she tries to find "someone who might listen. She had the Master's total voice in her head" (194).

Returning to the earlier matter of how to read the novel vis-à-vis its context, one might ask: is Karen a prototype of the cult member, an American

Christian equivalent to the frenzied Iranian mourners whom she watches on television as men pull down a helicopter so as to prevent it from taking their spiritual leader to his grave? *Mao II* is littered with such figures; even Bill Gray has fanatical readers (one sends him a severed finger in the mail). DeLillo has complicated this reductive view in interviews by noting of Karen that "I felt enormous sympathy toward Karen Janney, sympathy, understanding, kinship. I was able to enter her consciousness quickly and easily. And I tried to show this sympathy and kinship when writing from her viewpoint—a free-flowing, non-sequitur ramble that's completely different from the other characters' view-points. Karen is not especially likable. But once I'd given her a life independent of my own will, I had no choice but to like her—although it's simplistic to put it that way—and it shows in the sentences I wrote, which are free of the usual restraints that bind words to sentences in a certain way."[32]

One could cite a number of instances of Karen's antipathy (for instance, her initially defensive treatment of Brita). In most instances, however, the matter of perspective can be framed in terms of the Rushdie Affair. There is the matter of cultural sensitivity, for instance. In the opening pages, Karen recalls speaking in broken English to her Korean fellow cult members, assuming that they will understand her as a result. DeLillo is not a writer who allows political correctness to obstruct character development. (One could cite any number of Bill Gray's statements, or even the Lebanese terrorists' patronizing treatment of Brita in the final pages, as other examples.) A reader might forgive these by invoking the cultural conflict of the Rushdie Affair and claim DeLillo was asserting a rather abstract (and one might say puerile) notion of free speech. Such an assertion—or its other, which would be to dismiss the novel as racist, sexist, and the like—would approximate the manner in which Rushdie's critics and would-be assassins treated *The Satanic Verses:* as an orthodox screed rather than as a work of art. And in this case, a work of art that never allows the reader to step entirely away from either Karen's or Brita's point of view, either by way of the narration or the presence of the various paintings and photographs that are on and inside the book itself. In this other view, then, not only does DeLillo portray Karen's glossolalia, her desperately luminous perception of American urban life, and her fraught attraction to domineering patriarchal figures as more sensitive to the human complexity of history than not, but he also places the reader in a physical position through which to regard the world through Karen's eyes. When we "read" the novel from that perspective, we are placed in an abject relation similar to that in which tyrants place followers and victims when those tyrants use mass media to distort and deform the human sensorium. As noted in chapter 1, that abjection is a position that Susan Sontag criticized in her famous essay on Leni

Riefenstahl. In *Mao II,* however, Karen prevails over it by her own devices, the assumption being that the careful reader, viewing the novel through Karen's eyes, will do the same. As such, Karen returns to the world through art rather than against it. This is one perspective by which the novel regards its own designs and may fairly be said to reply to the Rushdie Affair.

The other perspective is that of Brita, a photographer working with a small grant to complete her project of photographing the world's great living writers. Bill Gray is the ultimate prize, as it had been decades since he was last seen in public or photographed. Brita's character appears to be partly inspired by Fay Godwin, whom William Weatherby describes in his 1990 book on the Rushdie Affair as a "professional photographer who specialized in portraits of writers, [and who] first photographed Salman Rushdie" in 1975 and again later as he was writing *The Satanic Verses.*[33] Just as Karen cannot be reduced to an easy allegory (rather, she complicates allegorical readings of the book), Brita's photographs of Bill Gray complicate any notion that he is an allegorical rendering of Salman Rushdie (or J. D. Salinger, the recluse who DeLillo claimed partly inspired the character) or even DeLillo himself. In this reading Brita's view of Bill Gray forms a part of what Peter Knight has described as the "repeated building up and undermining of equivalency in the novel."[34] We arrive then at the heart of *Mao II:* having complicated any quick allegory of it, we can begin to see that it is a mixed-media work made primarily of literary narrative but also with indispensable visual elements. As such it does not depict in some allegorical way the Rushdie Affair, or a cultural conflict, or a specific writer or crisis. Rather, it portrays the institution of the novel as it functions in an age in which it must compete with other media. Laura Barrett contends that *Mao II* "repeatedly affirms that no medium has a patent on truth or bears sole responsibility for the weightlessness of modern experience. Nor, for that matter, is any single medium capable of restoring order, a sentiment common to writers in the past half century."[35] One might take exception to the notion that the novel takes such a relative view of the matter, but every fiber of the novel's being, from its jacket design to its photographs and words, shakes with the burden of speaking for various media (understood in this sense, as the arts of literature, painting, and photography). In this view the novel's ensemble cast, most of whose perspectives the reader eventually inhabits, act as filters for the various channels by which artistic media point towards the truth. While that is the relative view, the novel is far more transparent with regard to another figure who stands in the way of that process: the modern terrorist.

Perhaps to reinforce the threat, DeLillo simplified the narration and sentences of *Mao II.* Genre is unclear. When brand names appear, they have a source, context, and a knowing observer, as when Scott regards the signs along Broadway. Gone also are the nominal "lists" of *White Noise;* so as to reinforce the point that Bill Gray is not a stand-in for DeLillo, Scott notes that "Bill was not a list-making novelist" (140). Certain lines (such as "just like Beirut") recur over the course of the novel, but they are scarce and emanate from random crowds.

The focus turns instead to the famed "speechiness" of DeLillo's characters to that end. Even in such cases when they offer discursions, the elaborate narrative apparatus of other novels is simplified so as to stress the common speech of characters in dialogue. The primary discursions involve the novelist Bill Gray's conversations with other characters. Bill discusses his seclusion when he first meets Brita to have his photos taken, invoking "doubt" (38) about it and his work ("doubt" being a term that also often appears in Weatherby's discussion of Rushdie's novel). In one of the most commonly cited passages from the novel, Bill describes "a curious knot that binds novelists and terrorists. In the West we become famous effigies as our books lose the power to shape and influence. Do you ask writers how they feel about this? Years ago I used to think it was possible for a novelist to alter the inner life of the culture. Now bomb-makers and gunmen have taken that territory. They make raids on human consciousness. What writers used to do before we were all incorporated" (41). The novel elaborates this line of thought in several different ways. There is the obvious allusion to the status of images in Islam. (At one point in the same scene Bill says, "In a mosque, no images.") Brita and Karen will each discuss aspects of Bill's ruminations on the novel, as well as his own photograph being taken, and they do so with each other, with others, or in the individual ways they think about photographs and paintings. Scott will focus most closely on the relationship between the author's image (literal and figural) when organizing Bill's papers later in the novel (during the course of which he offers a short biography of the writer). Bill's persistence after the topic is prompted perhaps by his gradual realization that a mere image will not suffice. He will discuss his options later with his friend and editor, Charlie Everson, after Bill agrees to meet with him in London to assist in the liberation of the Swiss poet.

Bill embarks on a journey that brings him closer to the prisoner, Julien. Bill abandons Karen and Scott, and he departs from his daughter. He leaves Charlie in London before the scheduled press conference and travels to Greece, where he meets again with George Haddad. Haddad, a professor of political science, is also a spokesman for the terrorist group that holds the poet hostage and the likely source of the leak that permitted the group to plant a bomb that explodes near Bill and Charlie in London (a scene that brings to mind bombings of British bookstores during the Rushdie Affair). As intellectual and also informant, Haddad represents the terrorists (who are not shown as such until the end of the novel, when their leader explains his cruel ideals to Brita and then watches serenely as his own son assaults her). In his exchange with Haddad in Greece, Haddad suggests that Bill might take his place—a possibility that has already been on Bill's mind. It is suggested that Bill may be taken involuntarily but for the problem of his transit across the Mediterranean, which is obstructed by the Lebanese civil war's disruption of sea routes. Meanwhile, Bill and George meet several times to discuss their ideas, their positions, and their options. During their conversations, George matches Bill's wit with his own intelligence and devotion to an ideal. What divides them, however, is their means. When Bill and George discuss the exchange, they talk about the fate of the prisoner and also his significance. For George his imprisonment is a poetic act designed to precipitate a coming political state. Responding to Bill's depiction of the imprisonment, George notes, "There are different ways in which words are sacred" (161). In George's view, people, and particularly the young, are vulnerable to the influence of words. The leader of a political movement must embody certain ideas and words so as to provide the young with a being to admire. George invokes Chairman Mao as the most relevant and admirable example. Bill responds: "Incantations. People chanting formulas and slogans" (162). By contrast, the young poet's mind represents a possibility to Bill, and a possibility that George's group, and every terrorist for that matter, would seek to annihilate along its dystopian march. In Bill's view, a "hostage is the miniaturized form" of "every closed state" (163). Their conversation is interrupted by small explosions in the city below, and then George offers his ultimatum: if Bill leaves Greece and returns to New York, George's group will kill the hostage poet.

In one of the novel's final chapters, Bill abandons George and leaves Greece for Cyprus with the intention of traveling by sea to Beirut. An old man who cleans the ship finds his corpse on the docked ship. To the man, Bill's papers may be valuable—not because he is a writer (the man does not know this) but because he is an American. He steals his papers to sell to militias who might use them, and Bill, who has died anonymously, vanishes from the book. The hostage poet's fate is also never revealed. There is no heroic death scene (the moments prior to Bill's death have a certain comedy about them, in fact), no final speech. A reader expecting a neat conclusion to Bill's story will perhaps be disappointed, as will the reader looking for some final allusion to the Rushdie Affair. Karen and Scott reunite and proceed with their caretaking of Bill's things, and Brita witnesses a wedding celebration during her final night while she is on assignment in Beirut, unaware of Bill's fate. Her photographs of Bill are not published. Placing the reader in a position to regard Bill through Karen's and Brita's eyes, DeLillo illuminates the novelist in the way that Warhol had illuminated the propaganda portrait of Chairman Mao; yet there is no literal effigy or portrait, apart from the words, the sentences, the novel.

A growing body of literary criticism has engaged DeLillo's depiction of artists and art. In a recent essay Peter Boxall concisely summarized the matter when he wrote, "In DeLillo's work, it might be argued, there is a refusal to distinguish between media culture and high culture, a refusal to discriminate, or exclude."[36] Boxall paraphrases the two points of view on the matter. In the first DeLillo appears to be an elemental postmodernist who has written his way into a corner in which literary fiction is trapped by its inability to do anything more than portray an inexorable and homogenous consumer culture. In the second view DeLillo's literary experiments result in exciting new ways to experience and reflect upon aesthetics within consumer culture while avoiding being entirely subsumed into that very same culture. Boxall concludes that there lies at the core of all the perceived commentary about DeLillo's work "a continued investment in David Bell's silence and darkness, by its location of a still point that cannot be brought into expression but from which his fiction emerges and toward which it is heading."[37] Referring to David Bell (the narrator of DeLillo's first novel *Americana*) in this way, Boxall describes the strange continuities of DeLillo's prose, continuities that vanish like the subterranean storylines of *White Noise,* only to reemerge again in some new context or form. If this is true, then *Mao II* is not perhaps so unique as I have made it to seem by comparison to DeLillo's other novels. It offers instead the most vivid glimpse of what Boxall describes as that "still point," at which, like Karen gazing upon the city, our sight translates into sound and what Bill Gray calls a "democratic shout" (159). That is the famous line, the sound bite, the sales pitch.

What do we miss in our selective readings of DeLillo's novels, as we trace patterns and lines, ferret for the proof of some idea? In the line that follows that famous phrase, Bill says, "Anybody can write a great novel, one great novel, almost any amateur off the street." The word "amateur" seems incongruous, a bad Francophone note wedged into Bill's wry American vernacular. "Amateur," signifying one who pursues an activity for pleasure rather than profit and who, as the root of the noun suggests, is motivated by love. An "*amatore,*" or one who loves. Love—it is not a word often associated with DeLillo or his novels.

CHAPTER 4

Artists and Prophets

The Body Artist, Cosmopolis, and *Falling Man*

A scene from Don DeLillo's novel *Falling Man* (2007) illustrates a salient narrative feature of the most recent phase of the writer's career. The scene in question opens the novel's seventh chapter. In it the character Lianne Glenn looks at a still-life painting hanging on the wall of her mother's New York City apartment. The painting draws her attention throughout the novel, but it assumes a new significance to Lianne in this scene. The narration, which shifts to Lianne's point of view, describes how the painting depicts "two dark objects, the white bottle, the huddled objects" (111). Lianne turns from the painting, and as she does so the painting extends out of its frame, into the room occupied by her mother, a retired art historian, and her mother's lover, an art dealer. Her name is Nina; his name is Martin. She was a professor at one time; prior to working as an art dealer, Martin was possibly involved in a militant left-wing group in his native Germany. The scene is suffused by the quiet tension between the figures in the painting and the figures in the room. Lianne ruminates on that tension and begins to interpret the painting. She describes how the two dark objects, which suggest the Twin Towers of the World Trade Center, cannot be allegorized. They cannot even be Nina and Martin. Set in the weeks following 9/11, the novel blurs the line between life and art at times; for example, a performance artist roams the city, re-creating the pose of a man who fell or jumped to his death from one of the burning buildings. Lianne, who refuses to admit any easy relationship between art and life in this moment, has begun to reclaim autonomy and perspective by thinking through the still-life painting, but also without simplifying, reducing, or dismissing the power of the art in question. Lianne appears to contradict the novelist Bill Gray in DeLillo's *Mao II* in that she refuses to admit that art can no longer shape the inner life of a culture. Only art, it would seem, has that conflicted privilege. Elaborating her daughter's discourse on the scene, Nina notes that the relationships in question—between art and history, persons and art, peoples—expose the delicate but persistent truth of what she calls "being human, being mortal" (111). As the scene concludes, the reader is left with the impression that the still life was alive, or coming to life, and that it was Lianne who made it so. Meaningful art does not appear from transcendent ideals; it is a restless point that stands out from a process of dialogue, thought, and deliberation. Lianne begins to process her trauma and gather a new life about her as a human being, citizen, and mother.

Clearly, this is not the fiction of alienation and despair that DeLillo is alleged to have exclusively written during the twentieth century. Sadness and solitude—or what remains of them—offer little defense against the new horror that has befallen Lianne's city. Only art offers sanctuary; literature speaks as its conscience. Read in light of this scene, the works of this most recent period of DeLillo's career appear more taciturn and introspective. It would be mistaken, however, to regard these writings as a mere reaction to the 9/11 attack, as DeLillo had written two of the novels in question—*Cosmopolis* and *The Body Artist*—prior to that day. The difference is in how his fiction articulates experiences and moods familiar to readers of his earlier work. Individual characters are not crowded by other figures, as they are in his earlier writings. With the exception of *Falling Man*, which effectively contrasts two protagonists (Lianne and Keith), the novels of this later period—*The Body Artist* (2001), *Cosmopolis* (2003), and *Point Omega* (2010)—dramatize individual lives with renewed attention to the affective intonations of words and characters. (Flashes of it were evident in earlier works, but largely ignored.) In these books the common themes and plot devices for which DeLillo was renowned (catastrophe, paranoia, consumerism) become minor props. The stages are sparse; characters communicate by elemental gestures; and the narration is more terse, syntactical relations more subtle (and also more refined, as we shall see). Lianne's perception of and response to the still-life painting embodies the point.

Some readers have expressed disappointment with DeLillo's recent novels. By contrast, I will argue that they rank as his most formally accomplished because in them he developed the narrative experiments of his earlier works in such a way as to amplify the dramatic and latent affective elements of his style. That section of DeLillo's audience that remains disaffected by these works can be excused for remaining in the fin-de-siècle twilight of novels such as *Underworld.* To some readers that novel is the high-water mark of DeLillo's career (as well as a certain phase of American literary fiction). Having composed three of the most celebrated novels of the late Cold War (*White Noise, Libra,* and *Mao II*), *Underworld* (1997) was DeLillo's second full-scale attempt at writing a historical romance (the first being *Libra*), and one that would take nothing less than the second half of the "American Century" as its subject. Rumored to have triggered a bidding war during which rights to the novel were sold for a six-figure sum (DeLillo denies this rumor, by the way), *Underworld* may be described as the publishing industry's version of the kind of "media event" that horrifies, stuns, and puzzles many of his fictional characters, regardless of its selling price. If Bill Gray's statement that novels changed "the inner life of a culture" can be transposed to the publishing event itself and thereby understood as the capital-intensive investment in the production and sale of literary fiction, then Gray was right insofar as the publication of *Underworld* legitimized literary postmodernism in the publishing mainstream on an unprecedented scale. It changed the culture: led by an astounding advertising "blitz" that included full-page ads in major newspapers and magazines, along with posters and displays that were distributed to booksellers, the novel's prepublication history was itself a media event; at the height of the frenzy, the world's best readers lined up to pay tribute (Salman Rushdie called it "magnificent") in glowing critical reviews. The buildup to *Underworld* resembled the chase for "the product" in *Great Jones Street:* it was an event that had escaped from one of DeLillo's plots.

A backlash of sorts developed against DeLillo, and postmodern literary fiction in general, in the years that followed the publication of *Underworld.* No reader could describe *Underworld* as a failure or as a sellout that compromised DeLillo's art. Had readers become exhausted by the promotional propaganda and hype that preceded it? Was it untimely insofar as it appeared in that very moment when the Cold War receded into memory and our attention was turned to the first signs of another historical phase, characterized by sectarian conflict, failed states, and the globalized flow of digital capital? Were its readers dulled to its achievement, victims of the repeated criticism that DeLillo's characters lacked "substance"? DeLillo had never written for critics, after all. Why write for critics, when you can write for crowds? These factors may have explained what happened in some way. Why read a historical novel, after all, after Frances Fukuyama (an intellectual aligned with DeLillo's more conservative critics) had declared the "end of history?"[1]

Wendy Steiner's essay "Look Who's Modern Now" (1999) encapsulates the backlash. In an argument that prefigures the recent critical turn toward lyrical postmodernism and postironic sentimentalism, Steiner's essay singled out *Underworld* as the poster child for a literary postmodernism that had run its course. While offering praise for the book's famous prologue, Steiner explained also that she (and other judges of the National Book Award Committee that year) had decided that DeLillo's well-written historical novel was nonetheless passé. The judges ruled in favor of another novel representing a "softer modernism," a work concerned not only with irony and despair but also with poetry and love. DeLillo's novel, by contrast, represented a male-dominated mode of literary fiction that had lost touch with the culture. A new fiction had taken its place, she argued, a fiction of "nurturing steadfastness" that augurs a return to sincerity.[2]

One might note a number of flaws in Steiner's argument. Why, for instance, had she excluded postmodernists such as Joan Didion and Kathy Acker from the accusation of "brittle intellectualism"? Did writers such as Toni Morrison or Louise Erdrich not qualify as "ethnic" or "traditional" or "postmodern" in some way? Steiner had published her essay in order to recant her survey of post–World War II American fiction in volume 7 of the *Cambridge History of American Literature* (1994). She had devoted the majority of that work to the same school of postwar American fiction to which DeLillo belonged, yet without excoriating it in that volume for its lack of feeling or cultural relevance. Indeed, her short account of DeLillo's *White Noise* in that volume is an excellent one; she praises it as "an especially apt case of contemporary fiction, in that it merges existentialism, politics and individual assertion" in a manner that joins the "Pynchonesque lion" of narrative technique with the "Rothian lamb" of "humanism."[3] Steiner's earlier argument had insightfully identified an oft-overlooked strain of affect in DeLillo's prose writings; her later argument singled out DeLillo and accused him of practice to the contrary. At the end of her polemical renunciation of DeLillo (and of a good deal of her previous work), she cited sales figures to partly justify the change of mind. Like history and the Cold War, literary postmodernism had also run its course, and the marketplace offered proof.

The Body Artist

Scribner, the publisher of all of DeLillo's new books beginning with *Underworld*, released *The Body Artist* in 2001.The original dust jacket of the first edition featured a detail from Michelangelo Caravaggio's *The Musicians*, but the subsequent paperback edition adopted a nude photographic portrait (cropped to eliminate the model's exposed breast) for its cover. The photograph was taken by the mid-twentieth-century photographer Bill Brandt. Its selection returned to the design style of the covers for DeLillo's prior novels. Previously, Viking printed *Mao II* with the eponymous painting by Andy

Warhol while Scribner had used André Kertész's 1972 photo of lower Manhattan, with a church steeple in the foreground and the Twin Towers of the World Trade Center, as the cover design for *Underworld.* The publisher chose in this case the work of a modern artist whose career was similar to DeLillo's own. Brandt had started his career in newspaper media and achieved renown with photographs of European cities (and London in particular) before and after World War II. During the 1940s and 1950s, he photographed portraits of modern artists including Pablo Picasso, Henry Moore, René Magritte, and Francis Bacon, as well as portraits of writers, among them Iris Murdoch, Dylan Thomas, and Graham Greene. (It should be noted these literary examples suggest an inspiration other than that of Fay Godwin for Brita's photographs of novelists in *Mao II.*) Thematically, the choice of Brandt's photo was perfect. Brandt's early works depicted a quasi-Victorian modern England, littered with advertisements and consumption, caught between two ages (think of the contrast between small-town America and big-time New York City in DeLillo's *Americana*). The quasi-neorealist photographs of landscapes and postwar urban ruins, as well as Brandt's experimental portraits of artists, suggest the postindustrial world of *White Noise.* Brandt's 1961 collection of photographs entitled *Perspectives on Nudes,* taken over a period of fifteen years, include some of the photographer's most celebrated images. The ironic portraits and empty landscapes of Brandt's historicist middle period give way to what Mark Haworth-Booth described as the "colossal scale" of Brandt's experiments with aesthetics and technique in the nudes of the period from which the cover of DeLillo's *The Body Artist* was drawn.[4]

One cannot help but note the suggestion offered by DeLillo's publisher: the choice of Brandt's photo for the first issue of *The Body Artist* in paper binding implies a similar aesthetic turn in DeLillo's career. In reproducing the work of a celebrated modern artist (DeLillo's affinity for modernism is well-known and widely discussed among his critics), the publisher associates DeLillo's latest work of fiction with Brandt's portraits. One might understand the cover in these biographical terms at some risk or note that publishers use such designs to invoke certain prestigious associations between their product and the jacket art in question. In a general sense, the covers adopt art as a type of visual shorthand in order to "recycle" the aesthetic modalities of an earlier historical time, thereby confirming a quintessential habit of postmodernism (which DeLillo portrays in a more cautious manner in his fiction). In any case, readers considering the selection of either the detail of Brandt's photo or that from Caravaggio's painting—both works of a decidedly more introspective mood—would have been right to expect that *The Body Artist* was somewhat different from DeLillo's previous novels.

The Body Artist begins with a short meditation on the passage of time. It is presumably offered in the second person as the pronoun "you" appears to address the reader. It then describes a morning scene. The set design is simple: a kitchen, two persons, and birds that appear outside the window. As the conversation begins, the narration turns from the second person to the third person with a series of personal pronouns in the third person—he, she, they—to establish preliminary dramatic roles. The third person alternates with first-person dialogue. Possessive pronouns—my, your—occasionally underscore tensions between persons and things, and are replaced at other times by articles—particularly "the"—which avoid possessive connotation. Pronouns accumulate a subtle tension as the chapter proceeds, and the tension serves to blur distinctions not only between person and objects but also between characters and readers. For example, when "he" (the reader has perhaps noted "she" calls him by name as "Rey" in a previous line) complains, she replies, "Give us all a break" (17), thereby using the oblique "us" to suggest a plurality. In a similar manner, the nominative "you" appears after he speaks, telling her, "You need the company" (21), but she has tuned him out. When the narration returns (presumably to her reading the paper), it does not adopt the third person but instead absorbs and elaborates his terse, even hostile use of "you." As in the opening paragraph of the chapter, the narration adopts the second person, using (or reusing) "you" again, but now it is unclear if the "you" refers to the reader or if it is a reflexive "you" by which she addresses herself. In a single sequence, the narration shifts from third-person pronouns describing her reading the paper to third-person narration describing him speaking in the first person, followed by a long paragraph using the oblique "you" to suggest the second person (which may also be her referring to herself), and finally returning to the third person ("she") to reestablish her point of view (or the reader's). Not only has the line between character and reader been blurred, but the distinction between the two characters has been destabilized by the shifts between gendered and ungendered pronouns, thereby serving early notice of a critical point in *The Body Artist.*

Whereas the words are crafted to impart the scrupulous syntactic attentions of poetry, the narrative stages the dialogue at a reflective pace. The mood is not only that of the subject's inner time, wherein time is not so much marked as interrupted and amplified by words (what Boxall calls "unmeasured time"). The technique resembles that of slow-motion cinematography, and it will appear again in the closing scene of DeLillo's *Cosmopolis* (2003), the opening sequence of *Falling Man* (2007), and as the operating principle of *Point Omega* (2010). As the narration proceeds, it assumes a modular, "stacked" quality, not unlike a cinematic montage. For example, rather than describing the birds outside the window in a single paragraph, DeLillo inserts references to them between other sections over the course of the opening chapter. These sequenced moments almost appear interchangeable, as if they could be restacked like dishes, but for the slow procession of inner, syntactical time that holds the dialogue in a tenuous chronological order.

An interchapter follows this first tour de force of literary prose. That chapter takes the form of a published obituary that describes the life and death of one of the two characters the reader had met in the book's poetic first chapter. The "she" of that chapter called him Rey. The obituary informs the reader that Rey Robles was a renowned director of avant-garde films, that his biography is not entirely clear, and that he has committed suicide. In the final lines we learn that he is survived by his wife—the novel's protagonist, the unnamed interlocutor who inhabits varied singular and plural pronouns in chapter 1—"Lauren Hartke, the body artist" (29).

Interchapters of this type are a common feature of DeLillo's novels. One thinks of the faux record-industry press releases he inserted between chapters of *Great Jones Street.* Yet they are integral rather than interruptive features of the later novels. DeLillo integrates the obituary at the beginning of *The Body Artist* and a later "published" review of Lauren's performance into the reflexive narrative structure of the book, blurring in unexpected ways the line between reader, narrator, and character. In the obituary interchapter, for instance, the reader is again returned to Lauren's point of view as a habitual reader of newspaper print, an implication that carries throughout the novel.

Modern mass media are a prominent feature of *The Body Artist.* Lauren and Rey share newspapers and listen to radio broadcasts. In DeLillo's previous novels, media play ambiguous and sinister roles in the lives of characters, but here their presence suggests shared imaginative currents, a communal and intimate media world. Using conjunctions to imply the point, DeLillo writes in the first chapter: "You separate the Sunday sections and there are endless identical lines of print with people living somewhere in the words and the strange contained reality of print seeps through the house and when you look at a page and distinguish one line from another it begins to gather you into it and there are people being tortured halfway around the world, who speak another language, and you have conversations with them more or less uncontrollably until you become aware that you are doing it and then you stop, seeing whatever it is in front of you at the time, like half a glass of juice in your husband's hand" (19). In a recent study, Tyler Kessel has claimed that such moments confirm the "textualization of Lauren," but if the reader is willing to accept Kessel's claim, then it can be extended to a "textualization" of the reader as well.[5]

Using the smallest parts of speech to great poetic effect and then extending their subtle narration to the implied reader(s) of the first interchapter, the opening pages of *The Body Artist* are unique in DeLillo's career. One might compare them to the "memorable" opening scenes of so many of his novels. But where those famous scenes experiment with perspective on a macrocosmic scale, *The Body Artist* reverses the scale. Yes, there is a comparable complexity, but *The Body Artist* shifts the burden of that complexity to the smallest units of human communication: words. The difference is that between astrophysics and poetry. It asserts furthermore DeLillo's devotion to the medium of print. It is as though the narration had suddenly become aware of another layer of texture, a more porous and malleable medium that allows the writer to integrate other media and genres (such as the obituary and performance review) into its substance to more subtle effect. A certain distance will eventually return with the second interchapter—the book is not a painting, this is not a pipe—yet the distance between writer and medium, character and reader, has effectively vanished.

The Body Artist also integrates another, more recent medium into this dynamic: the Internet. In her grief after Rey's suicide, Lauren begins impulsively to watch a live web camera that broadcasts images from a Finnish highway. It replaces her prior relationship to newspapers, yet without the dialogue of community. It breeds solipsism rather than solace. The new medium engrosses her and she recedes into her grief. She begins a regimen of exercises, working almost mechanically, to prepare for a nebulous performance whose form has not yet become clear in her mind. Suspended in this mournful state, Lauren finds "him" in the house.

She eventually gives him a name, "Mr. Tuttle," and she imagines at one point that he has materialized out of the computer. Lauren resents his presence at first, fearing it because she imagines he may be a homeless man or a patient escaped from a psychiatric hospital. (The latter is eventually implied as a probable explanation.) Mr. Tuttle ultimately poses no physical threat to her. He is childlike, innocent (but not entirely), suggesting a more subtle and articulate version of Mrs. Micklewhite's wailing son in *Great Jones Street*. Peter Boxall has perceptively noted that the two characters share many common features in that both are "naked, prehistorical" figures. Boxall also notes that Lauren, in preparing her performance, will "enter Mr. Tuttle's continuum, where past, present, and future are distinctions that have not yet been devised."[6] The difference between Bucky and Lauren, and *Great Jones Street* and *The Body Artist*, lies in the manner by which Mr. Tuttle is introduced after the breaking down of narrative distinctions and through Lauren's orientation to the new medium of the Internet (as a medium of introspection rather than alienation). In *Great Jones Street,* the combined narration and characterization are not afforded a comparably refined attention.

Lauren attributes to Mr. Tuttle the strange noises that she had previously heard in the old coastal New England house. The reader may recall the hair she found in the first chapter, a clue that reinforced our shared point of view with Lauren. She concludes that Mr. Tuttle has been there for some time and that, more important, he has been listening. Like Lauren or the blue jay that is described as a "a skilled mimic" (22) in chapter 1, Mr. Tuttle repeats what he hears. Yet while he has a capacity for mimesis, he does not appear able to coordinate the relationship between the words he imitates with time. Lacking context or a register for the nonverbal cues of communication, he speaks without self-awareness. He completely lacks irony. Lauren soon recognizes that Mr. Tuttle speaks with her late husband's words and intonations. Mr. Tuttle had listened to recordings of Rey, who had dictated his autobiography into a tape recorder.

In the middle sections of the novel, Lauren begins interviewing Mr. Tuttle and recording his interviews with the same tape recorder Rey had used. She observes his manner and speech, and she begins to imitate him (and, by default, her dead husband). The novel begins to fold back on itself in time. Earlier lines of dialogue assume new significance as language synchronizes in a mimetic loop. The novel has already described what she is doing in an earlier passage that extends the description of reading the newspaper to her final moments with Rey: "You become someone else, doing dialogue of your own devising. You become a man at times, living between the lines, doing another version of the story" (20).

In the fifth chapter of the novel, Lauren realizes that Mr. Tuttle repeats her final conversation with Rey prior to Rey's suicide. The reader does not know until this point that the last scene of the first chapter is also the last of their marriage: after the morning breakfast, Rey drives to New York City and kills himself. Lauren has been all the while training by stretching muscles, trimming hair, and scouring pores in preparation for a performance. She has found its subject—"you"—in and through Mr. Tuttle. The main section of the novel concludes.

The main section of the book consists of the five chapters in which Lauren discovers, observes, and becomes Mr. Tuttle. These are followed by the second interchapter. It takes the form of an article, part performance review and part interview, written by Lauren's college roommate, a journalist named Mariella. To this point DeLillo has fused the novel in a sequence of delicate metaphors (Lauren–Rey–Blue Jay–Tuttle–You) and chronological folds. Mariella's article adds a new texture in that it is the first time in which media introduce a distancing and objective communication in the novel. Mariella's summary of Lauren's performance describes the characters that Lauren mimics in her art. The reader recognizes them from earlier chapters. Lauren sees an "ancient" Japanese woman in town (and sees her again in the final chapter, as Lauren considers revising her work). The live webcam of the highway in Kotka, Finland, plays behind her on the stage. She becomes Mr. Tuttle and also Rey, a physical mimicry of the voices on the tape recorder. Lauren acts only with her body, translating words into gesture and movement (or stillness). Mariella, the journalist, also appears (as a voice recording) in the performance from an earlier scene in which she speaks with Lauren over the telephone. A final question includes a miniature of the entire novel to that point, yet it is part of Mariella's article rather than the performance: when Mariella asks whether Rey's suicide inspired Lauren's performance, Lauren denies any link. And then Lauren begins speaking to Mariella in Mr. Tuttle's voice (as Rey). The artistic performance, and all of its prior confusions between physical and verbal language, erupt from the article's condensed recitation of the novel itself. Mariella describes her reaction: "It is about you and me. What begins in solitary otherness becomes familiar and even personal. It is about who we are when we are not rehearsing who we are" (109–10). Mariella has effectively been absorbed into the narrative, which is not a novel at this point so much as a physical performance imitated in words (and vice versa). We see the repetition by perceiving Mariella's distance from what we have read in the previous pages. The distance is not one between reader and text, however, but rather between reader and varied narrative modes (journalism, fiction) that have unique narrative modes and capacities. Even as the reader reviews the novel in light of Mariella's article, Mariella's review returns us to the world of print.

Lauren returns instead to the old house after her performance. Mr. Tuttle is gone. The tactile comforts of other routines return to comfort her. One routine does not. Lauren notes, "She hadn't read a paper in a long time" (115). Suspended in the timeless present of her work, her art, Lauren dissociates from the world. She has visions of Rey, her work, and herself (the reflexive pronoun emerges with emphasis in the book's final pages). She speaks to herself and to the reader, but not as the reader, as if to say, in the didactic sentiment of the novel's final lines, that it is print that divides us and art that brings us together. As is often the case in DeLillo's novels, the conclusion avoids any simple resolution. The verb tenses of the novel's final lines suggest the complexity of how Lauren desires experience and self-awareness even as she seeks sensations and temporalities that will "tell her who she was." With elusive pronouns and contrasting verb tenses, DeLillo concludes *The Body Artist* so as to break the narrative bond that joins the reader to Lauren.

DeLillo's academic readers have offered a mixed view of *The Body Artist.* In a 2011 study, Paul Giaimo claims that the novel "yields a look at the concept that the artist's first moral responsibility is to his or her integral self." Giaimo then describes Lauren's dead husband, Rey, as an inhibiting and repressive presence that Lauren must shed in order "to live healthfully and successfully as an artist." Discussion concludes with "moving on to wider spheres, 2007's *Falling Man,*" suggesting that *The Body Artist* had been in some way a minor and provincial exception to the main body of DeLillo's works.[7]

Peter Boxall has taken a more subtle and compelling view of DeLillo's postmillennial fiction. He devotes the final chapter of his excellent 2006 study *Don DeLillo: The Possibility of Fiction* to it, describing DeLillo's characters of the period as inhabiting "unmeasured time." Boxall discusses both *The Body Artist* and *Cosmopolis* (his book appeared in the year before *Falling Man*) to show how DeLillo's sense of narrative time (as well as our own) "has escaped from its boundaries, and is no longer measured in decades." Invoking the "out-of-joint" time of Shakespeare's *Hamlet,* Boxall describes the postmillennial turn in DeLillo's writing: "One of the working contradictions of DeLillo's most recent prose [is] that this evacuation of the moment, this entry into the suspended non-time of post-historical mourning, is also a delivery into the very fibrous material of the moment itself." Boxall proceeds to draw an insightful comparison between *The Body Artist* and *Americana,* novels that he claims share an ambition to transform how readers experience a novel. According to Boxall, *Americana* was forward-looking, but a novel that looked to the end of a certain way of enumerating historical time in literary-narrative terms; *The Body Artist* is instead a novel that erases the threshold in question and explores alternately the narrative possibilities of that aforementioned "unmeasured time." The question remains, however, of whether *The Body Artist*'s unmeasured time does not also betray a new historicity; Boxall believes that it does, using the role of the Internet (the novel's Finnish webcam) to make his point. Boxall's argument makes a persuasive case for how *The Body Artist* challenges the reader to reconsider not only its writer's gifts but the role that literary narrative might play in and against our evolving notions of "unmeasured time" and history.[8]

Cosmopolis

Boxall's description of *The Body Artist* and its successor *Cosmopolis* (2003) as elaborating "unmeasured time" indicates a shift in the historical orientation of DeLillo's fiction, and the reader should not regard that shift as something amorphous, ahistorical, or abstract. Nor should the two novels in question be regarded as identical. As I sought to illustrate in my summary of *The Body*

Artist, DeLillo's careful attention to the tenses and voicing of words imparted to that work a narrative subtlety unmatched by his previous writings. One might say it even affirms the continuing narrative power of print media into—and against—the Internet Age. Furthermore, the novel's narrative elements are perfectly interwoven with its dramatic characters and events, so much so that they are inseparable parts of what is arguably his most complete work of literary fiction. *The Body Artist* uses time and tense to synchronize the relationships that bond the audience, artist, and the work of art. In *Cosmopolis* the narration instead dramatizes asynchronous temporalities that torment consumers, financiers, and global capital markets.

The narrative principles shared by the two novels are quite simple. *The Body Artist* used parts of speech such as pronouns and verbs to transfer agency between and among characters and audiences. (DeLillo uses pronouns in that way to a different effect in the closing pages of *Cosmopolis.*) Placed at strategic intervals in *The Body Artist,* the protean words slowly create a web of mimetic displacements whose primary movement is cohesive. Time is understood there as a linear sequence of actions and reactions that slow to a dreamlike and ultimately recursive form as gestures imitate words and vice versa. Time is not so much disrupted as it is folded back on itself to expose nonsequential trajectories of memory, language, and gesture. It is "fibrous," to use Boxall's term, in that it develops the textured integrity of an aesthetic form that embodies Lauren's artistic becoming. In this way *The Body Artist* dramatizes a shared human time in which language attains a malleable and unifying materiality.

Cosmopolis reconfigures the temporal arrangements of *The Body Artist.* In the latter work pronouns diffused dramatic roles, thereby connecting the audience with Lauren's tactile sense of time and language. In *Cosmopolis,* by contrast, DeLillo introduces language that moves at light speed. Transitions are abrupt and every detail and word quickly loses depth; narrative time is asynchronous with respect to human language, sensuality, and perception. Whereas *The Body Artist* opened the density of narrative time, *Cosmopolis* dramatizes its electrified disruption.

Yet DeLillo's execution of a narrative organization in *Cosmopolis* is as complex and artful as that of *The Body Artist.* The primary difference is in the dramatic result: whereas the latter novel's characters cohere in time, the characters of *Cosmopolis* literally come apart. The novel's protagonist, Eric Packer, reacts to the video of an explosion before a bomb actually explodes outside his car. In a later scene he sees video of his murdered body being wheeled into a morgue, even though he is still alive. An assassin describes the same death scene from his own point of view, but several chapters before the murder actually occurs. Eric never truly dies in the novel, although his death is described to the reader by two different characters (one being the presumed deceased). In this way the novel uses anachronism and discontinuity to dramatize the asynchronous time of global capital markets: Eric expires but he does not. Rather, he continues to exist as a numerical quantity on a spreadsheet, in the form of debt, as an image broadcast for media consumption, as a shock wave washing over collapsing global markets, and so on. In the words of Eric's Chief of Theory, Vija Kinski, Eric inhabits an economy in which "people will not die" (104).

As noted in previous chapters, DeLillo has written often about American business culture. Advertising, publishing, contraband, waste disposal, art, entertainment, and academia count among the economic activities to which he devotes long sections of earlier novels. Signs of these activities can intrude on every second of our lives and even saturate our consciousness (let alone our sleep, as is the case in *White Noise*). In DeLillo's America there is a business person for every artist or assassin and a dollar to be made for every second of our attention, divided or otherwise. While DeLillo has often discussed contemporary market capitalism, *Cosmopolis* is his only novel since *Players* (1977) devoted almost entirely to the portrayal of American financial markets. John McClure presciently observed in a 1991 essay that for DeLillo, "capitalism has penetrated everywhere, but its globalization has not resulted in global rationalization and Weber's iron cage."[9] As McClure notes, DeLillo's early novels looked to spaces at the edges of empires to identify exceptions to globalization. *Cosmopolis* instead ventures into New York City, the heart of global capital during the final days of the twentieth century.

Specifically, *Cosmopolis* dramatizes the international currency markets, markets that Eric Packer has manipulated in order to become the most powerful investor on the planet. The world is his office. His office is mobile, unmoored, because the majority of the novel takes place inside or in close proximity to Eric's limousine. The automobile is a character in its own right. Armor-plated, it is decorated with marble floors and fitted with cameras that provide a 360 degree view from its interior. Where Lauren Hartke exists *in* an expansive, open-ended time, Eric Packer is contained in the limousine by quantified simulations of time that scroll along the limousine's computer monitors.

In structure *Cosmopolis* consists of four chapters and two interchapters. Chapter 1 opens the novel in Eric Packer's luxury New York triplex, where Eric does not awaken so much as he transitions from insomnia to work. He leaves the building to find his limousine, driver, and security detail waiting for him on the street. A fictional American president named Midwood is visiting the city on that day, and the midtown traffic patterns have been altered. Eric's primary goal, while working from his limousine, is to make his way across town to get a haircut. The scenes that follow alternate between planned meetings and fortuitous encounters. The majority involve people who work for Eric, characters who are picked up along the streets. The characters include his director of technology, his chief currency officer, and his finance officer. Eric sometimes leaves them in the car, after which they vanish from the narrative or are suddenly replaced by a new character when Eric returns to the limousine. These characters function as advisors to Eric's main financial strategy: to "bet" against the devaluation of the Japanese yen and to profit thereby. Eric insists its value will not rise, he ignores his advisors, and the yen increases in value over the course of the single day in which the novel is set.

Unlike the recursive episodes of *The Body Artist,* the scenes in *Cosmopolis* have a cumulative effect. Minor anachronisms gather along the novel's course and move toward some final event. For instance, Eric meets with his "Chief of Theory," a company officer named Vija, at midday in Times Square. The limousine, which is again caught in traffic, is surrounded there by a crowd of rioting anarchists protesting the U.S. president's visit (among other things). Inside the limousine Eric and Vija watch from monitors as the riot unfolds while they discuss the relationship between currency and time. Vija tells Eric, "The present is harder to find. It is being sucked out of the world to make way for the future of uncontrolled markets and huge investment potential. The future becomes insistent" (79). Moments later, Eric recoils *before* a bomb detonates beside the limousine. In Vija's world, wherein technology accelerates time, the future is already in the present. In his arrogance Eric does not yet understand that the anachronistic effect may apply to him.

Eric punctuates the ironic anachronisms of the novel's narration by offering a running commentary on technological obsolescence. Obsolescence is not limited to technology; Eric extends it to human beings as well. He often describes and reflects upon objects, customs, and ideas that he regards as uselessly archaic. Automated teller machines are "so cumbrous and mechanical that even the acronym seemed outdated" (54). He imagines cash registers "confined to display cases in a museum of cash registers in Philadelphia or Zurich" (71). Offices, sleep, telephones, computers, and even ethnicity are all obsolete in his eyes. What Eric does not yet recognize is that he too is becoming a reliquary human form displaced by the very technologies he claims to master. While Eric appears proud and cynical in the novel's early chapters, his inner life becomes increasingly thoughtful and complicated. He contemplates poetry and admires abstract art (regarding the latter also as an investment). He wants to love his wife, the poet Elise Shifrin, who regards Eric with suspicion and expresses her reservations to him. They meet at random throughout the novel, and they finally communicate during a final encounter. Even as Eric becomes sympathetic and thoughtful, he remains enthralled by the very same technology that makes him obsolete. After speaking with Elise in a final, poignant scene, Eric punches a few buttons and drags her finances (she is a wealthy heiress) into the whirlpool that pulls him "out of the world," thereby rendering him the very sort of anachronism—a fallible human being—that he regards with contempt.

Cosmopolis appeared at a specific moment in the history of American capital and technology. It is a world of volatile financial transactions quickened by the rapidity of digital communications. Those digital networks of communication resemble those that Bill Gates described in his 1999 book *Business @ the Speed of Thought.* A primer on how to build (or rebuild) industry so as to synchronize it with emergent digital technologies, Gates's book draws upon the examples of major multinational corporations (Microsoft, Boeing, and others) to illustrate his practical advice. For example, the book's fifteenth chapter, entitled "Big Wins Require Big Risks," describes how Boeing, the aerospace company, streamlined a "digital information flow" to facilitate and also accelerate communication between its Japanese and American offices.[10] Equipped with a glossary of terms for the digital media ingénue (presumably the "old guard" of executives and managers who resisted the new technologies), Gates's book is part prophecy, part assembly manual.

The metaphoric subtitle of Gates's book is *Using a Digital Nervous System,* and Gates uses that cerebral metaphor to illustrate business communications in the new digital economy. According to Gates, institutional hierarchies old and new must learn to exchange information between their respective offices (such as finance, design, manufacture, marketing, and sales). In Gates's words, a fully integrated corporation becomes like "the human nervous system. The biological nervous system triggers your reflexes so that you can react quickly to danger or need. It gives you the information you need as you ponder issues and make choices. You're alert to the most important things, and your nervous system blocks out the information that isn't important to you."[11] The operating assumption of this metaphor is one of unwavering optimism with respect to the vigilant system's infallible communications.

Cosmopolis portrays a world in which the new digital communications systems are more pervasive than they appear to be in Gates's book (which was published in 1999, one year prior to the one in which *Cosmopolis* is set). Eric's investment company was nonetheless the prototypical start-up of the new world of 1990s digital finance. The novel informs the reader that his company first took form as a website "forecasting stocks" (75), after which it grew into a global powerhouse. Having established a corporate structure based upon a model of communication similar to that described by Gates (and represented in the novel by the various officers of the company), Eric Packer quickly became the most powerful investor on the planet. He soon found himself mingling with Russian tycoons, I.M.F. officers, and an American president, to mention a few examples of his social circle. (I use the word "social" loosely, as the characters inhabit virtual fortresses and have little social interaction of which to speak beyond the media and work.) As such, from its human networks to its business communications, the world that is contemporary with *Cosmopolis* is that which Gates described, the difference being one of scale; the individual "nervous systems" of Gates's varied multinational corporations have become a single system: the global capital market.

In the view of Vija Kinski, Eric's Chief of Theory, that market has attained a universal presence with the capacity to rationalize financiers as well as their rioting opponents. In her view, the market's growth has inexorable momentum capable of absorbing and commodifying everything, including resistance. Eric, however, senses another possibility within the market's increasing speed and expanding mass: an exception to the market's near totality. The exception appears to Eric while he and Vija watch the riot from within the limousine. They watch on the computer monitors as a protestor immolates himself in the square outside: "'What did this change?' . . . 'Everything,' he thought. Kinski had been wrong. The market was not total. It could not claim this man or assimilate his act" (99–100). Realizing that the market was fallible, Eric hedges his bets against it, attempting thereby to exploit what he presumes to be the market's weakness: an exceptional individual. Eric persuades himself that he is the Wall Street analog of the self-immolating man: a nervous system that the market cannot control or direct. Insist as Eric might upon his own counterintuitive pride, the Japanese currency rises in value against his judgments and prognostications.

In the end, Eric Packer would seem the ironic victim of his own disgust for obsolete things. He loses his bet but in actuality he becomes the victim of another outsider: a homeless man. Using the pen name of Benno Levin, the homeless man writes a journal, the chapters of which constitute the interchapters of *Cosmopolis*. Benno Levin, we learn, is a former employee of Eric's company, and his real name is Richard Sheets. Writing as Benno Levin in two interchapters, Levin/Sheets describes his employment at Eric's investment firm, his failed marriage, and his current life as an occupant of an abandoned building. Levin/Sheets also makes a brief appearance in an early chapter, when Eric notes a "familiar" man (54) standing near an ATM machine. In the first of the interchapters from the diary recounted by Levin, the reader also sees Eric, not as a man in a limousine near the ATM, however, but as a corpse on the floor. In this way, the narrative structure of *Cosmopolis* embeds anachronisms (Eric's premature reaction to the explosion, Levin's description of his corpse, and so forth) within its plot.

The novel's chronological disruptions are largely an effect of the narration's organization, which is slightly out of sequence. These disruptions are most obvious in the Levin interchapters, although the reader may not realize it while reading them (whereas in *The Body Artist* the attentive reader becomes aware, rather than forgetful). As in *The Body Artist,* DeLillo elaborates narrative along a temporal axis, modifying it in different ways to dramatize the novel's characters and milieu. In the earlier novel, narrative time becomes malleable. It is not so much amorphous as it is pliant. Just as Lauren can make her physical appearance and gestures into those of a man, the attentive reader can learn to inhabit the narrative, only to follow Eric into ruin. Time, in this sense, is a mimetic element that takes a physical form in art, as art that must be attained by a certain imaginative discipline. (DeLillo's admiration for asceticism takes its most daring aesthetic form in this case.) *Cosmopolis* also works along a temporal axis, modifying it to dramatize the novel's characters and milieu. But whereas narrative time becomes malleable in the earlier novel, it hardens into violence—the rigor of Eric's corpse—in the later book. The time of markets is the time of quantities, of physical presence reduced to an inanimate state. The reader cannot participate, only observe and await the next turn. Time, in this sense, is a mimetic element that is repeatedly invaded and deformed by the false nervous systems of markets and their surrogate machines, against any willful resistance. (DeLillo's suspicion of global markets takes its most critical form in this case.)

Despite differences that render the two novels distinct, the final chapter of *Cosmopolis* briefly returns to the semantic ambiguities that worked as the poetic narrative material of *The Body Artist.* In the final scene Eric accompanies his limousine to its parking lot. A shot rings out from an empty building across the street. Eric enters the empty building and confronts Benno Levin/Richard Sheets. Pronouns blur the line between Benno and Eric, as well as Eric and his own corpse, as he witnesses his own death (187, 197). In *The Body Artist,* the anachronistic pathos of language includes the willing reader; in *Cosmopolis* the anachronistic force of language renders the reader powerless to save its victims. In the former, we are both the audience and characters, whereas in the latter we are confused spectators at an execution.

Reviewers and academic critics responded to *Cosmopolis* in very different ways, so much so that *Cosmopolis* appears distinct in the history of criticism about DeLillo's writings. Academics have since championed the novel as one of DeLillo's most accomplished books, whereas reviewers initially compared it unfavorably to DeLillo's earlier writings (and to *Underworld* in particular). But reviewers also judged *Cosmopolis* in relation to the terrorist attacks of September 11, 2001, a world historical media event to which they expected the novel to reply in some way. This is because *Cosmopolis* was Don DeLillo's first novel to be published after the murderous spectacle of September 11, 2001. In the nearly two years that passed between that day and the publication of *Cosmopolis* (and nearly continuously thereafter), reviewers increasingly turned DeLillo into a prophet of sorts, an artist who had since *White Noise* best described how we react to terror, disaster, and genocide. In a sense reviewers and writers painted DeLillo as being possessed by a literary variant of Eric Packer's ability to witness a fateful event before its occurrence.

Reviewing *Cosmopolis* in the *Guardian,* author Blake Morrison asked: "Is *Cosmopolis* a post–September 11 novel? Yes and no. When the planes hit the twin towers 20 months ago, it looked like something from DeLillo, and having got there before it happened he's surely right not to revisit the scene. But the omens are present [in *Cosmopolis*]." In a 2005 essay published in the *New York Times Book Review,* Benjamin Kunkel struck the same note when writing about literary depictions of terrorism published during the 1990s: "No one has been more explicit or intelligent about all this [literature that mixes 'detestation of the terrorist with a distinct if shameful envy'] than Don DeLillo."[12] In an earlier section of the article, Kunkel reaches back to DeLillo's 1977 novel *Players* to cite a line from that novel that describes the "transient" properties of the Twin Towers of the World Trade Center, thereby setting a precedent for DeLillo's prophetic appearance.[13] The depiction of DeLillo as a postmodern seer continued through Michiko Kakutani's review of DeLillo's subsequent novel, which depicted characters in post-9/11 New York City, as the review begins with the statement: "No writer has been as prescient and eerily prophetic about 21st century America as Don DeLillo."[14] Reviewers extended the prophetic trope in a new direction when director David Cronenberg's film adaptation of *Cosmopolis* was released in 2012. In this case they regarded DeLillo as a prophet of another event: the 2007 global recession prompted by banks, predatory lenders, and market speculators. Returning to that novel in a film review published in the *Los Angeles Review of Books,* Cornel Bonca wrote: "Re-reading *Cosmopolis* now, . . . given the context of the 2007 global meltdown and the Occupy movement that followed, it appears to me that DeLillo has once again taken on the mantle of the artist-prophet."[15]

In these reviews and others, to borrow Peter Boxall's terms, it is as though the "smallest warps and discontinuities" of DeLillo's recent novels had somehow escaped into the world and visited DeLillo's reviewers. Again, one reconsiders Bill Gray's statement in *Mao II* in which the character—a novelist —remarks that novelists can no longer shape the "inner life of a culture." I do not criticize the reviewers' anachronisms here. One can reasonably admit that DeLillo's fiction has shaped the way in which we respond to traumatic world-historical violence and disaster. It was also reasonable to expect that DeLillo, who is after all a proud New Yorker, would respond to the savagery committed against his native city in some way. (We will visit his post-9/11 essay, as well as his belated post-9/11 fiction, later in this chapter.) It is confirmation that novels can still shape our sensibility in ways that ask us to feel and think anew. One can obtain perspectives and influences far worse.

If there is a criticism to be made, it is that in shaping the discussion of DeLillo's more recent fiction in prophetic terms, criticism also limited the ability of reviewers to recognize the sensational narrative achievements of his recent novels. There was little precedent for them to follow, as DeLillo's enemies had complained about his "flat" characters for decades. The trend continued through his recent works. Denby offered a favorable review of the film. After the reference to Updike's critique of DeLillo's novel, Denby defended both the book and its adaptation when he wrote that "when John Updike reviewed the novel [*Cosmopolis*] in these pages, he asked why we should care about the possible death of this arrogant cipher," that "arrogant cipher" being Eric Packer, of course.[16] The premise of such criticism is that a protagonist must be "sympathetic" and that the story must communicate a moral virtue. In Updike's view it is possible to praise a novel only if it conforms to a certain set of moral conventions that are embodied in its principal character or characters. Here, too, we find another sort of anachronism, not a prophetic one that imposes contemporary criteria on DeLillo's past writings but an absolutism of the metaphysical variety.

Cosmopolis was greeted in a much different manner by DeLillo's academic readers. As noted earlier, Peter Boxall's 2006 study is exemplary in that it distinguishes DeLillo's later fiction while not losing sight of its relationship to the earlier writings. By contrast, reviewers such as Kakutani (writing about *Falling Man*) and Morrison (writing about *Cosmopolis*) unfavorably compared the respective novels to DeLillo's *Underworld*. Their frame of reference was divided between prophecy and the past, allowing little room for any new relation to the present time (or, for that matter, the future).

Boxall, a British intellectual, counts among an influential group of academic critics who have revitalized discussion of DeLillo's writings of the young millennium. They include both American and British writers. Some are renowned scholars of DeLillo's work who were part of the first wave of DeLillo's academic readers during the late 1980s. They include figures such as John McClure, Mark Osteen, John T. Duvall, David Cowart, and others. In recent years other established literary intellectuals have also turned to DeLillo's writings. They include Stacey Olster, Joseph Conte, Patrick O'Donnell, and Linda S. Kaufman, the last of whom has published a series of excellent writings on *Falling Man,* as we shall see. Critics of more recent vintage, such as Boxall, Phillip Nel, and Tim Engles, have also published excellent recent criticism on DeLillo's writings, with increased attention to his recent fiction. While their publications are dispersed in monographs and academic journals, these critics, together with others, have also contributed original essays that appeared in two recent collections devoted to DeLillo's writings: *The Cambridge Companion to Don DeLillo* (2008) and *Don DeLillo:* Mao II, Underworld, Falling Man (2011). The latter volume features only passing references to *Cosmopolis,* while the former volume devotes substantial sections, as well as an entire essay, to that novel.[17] The sections include John McClure's discussion of DeLillo's sense of mystery in a theological key, dividing attention between his Catholicism and "ecstatic traditions."[18] Ruth Helyer explains instead masculinity, violence, and the media in her discussion of the novel,[19] while Peter Knight's essay explains DeLillo's novel in the context of Fredric Jameson's notion of "late capitalism."[20]

Joseph Conte's fine essay in that volume, which is devoted entirely to *Cosmopolis,* merits discussion for the careful attention that Conte pays to the difficulty of calibrating *Cosmopolis* in relation to the terrorist attack of September 11, 2001 (and perhaps by extension, but perhaps with greater relevance, to the economic crisis of 2007). Conte begins by noting that DeLillo had "nearly finished drafting his thirteenth novel, *Cosmopolis* (2003), at the time" and that DeLillo subsequently stepped away from the work after September 11, 2001.[21] Reviewing the temptation to regard DeLillo's prose as prophetic, the essay is careful to note the tendency but does not succumb to it. Conte chooses instead to draw a contrast between the novel and event: "In millennial American culture, the catastrophe of the Towers seizes on consciousness, its terror breaking through the anomie of multinational capitalism and media saturation."[22]

Disruption results in a sudden transformation of historical perspective, a paradigmatic shift in which we regard global capital—a quasi monopoly that replaces the binary conflicts of the Cold War—as having generated a new antagonist (terror) from within its own design. The result, explained in part through the persistence of American Cold War–era intellectuals (the neoconservatives) who framed the "War on Terror" by recycling the familiar rhetoric of the Cold War, transforms what appeared at first as a paradigmatic shift into a sort of tragic repetition. In Conte's view it is unfair to regard *Cosmopolis* as a literary reply to 9/11. Rather, he argues that the terror of 9/11 is best understood as a horrifically violent response to the global markets depicted in *Cosmopolis* and in an indirect way also an attack against the secular traditions of individualism, democracy, and literary expression represented by the institution of the modern novel.

One might ask, at such a point, why DeLillo felt compelled eventually to write a novel that would depict in some way the 9/11 attack and its aftermath. After all, if one agreed with reviewers who claimed him a prophet of the event, it would seem that he had already written about 9/11 before the fact (for example, in Brita's running commentary in *Mao II* regarding the Twin Towers' proximity to her apartment in lower Manhattan).

Scribner published Don DeLillo's fourteenth novel, entitled *Falling Man,* in 2007. The novel was received with confusion and dismay. Reviewing it in the *New York Times,* Michiko Kakutani coupled the book with its predecessor: "Unfortunately, his strangely stilted 2003 novel 'Cosmopolis' was a terrible disappointment, and so is his spindly new novel, 'Falling Man.'" Reviewing *Falling Man* in the *New York Review of Books,* critic Andrew O'Hagan asked, "What becomes of a prophet when his word becomes deed?" O'Hagan proceeds to draw attention to the novel's sentences, which he believes to be of a lesser quality, describing them as examples of DeLillo's "inability to conjure his usual exciting prose." Is it fair to expect a person, who as Conte notes was so affected by the attack that he stopped working, to compose an excited response to such an event? Reviewers expected perhaps a "mega-novel," along the lines of *Underworld* or *White Noise,* and O'Hagan is correct to note a scene in *Falling Man* that regards the notion of such a book with suspicion and distaste. With *Falling Man,* reviewers implied, Don DeLillo refused to come down the mountain.

When read in light of *The Body Artist* and *Cosmopolis,* however, *Falling Man* would seem consistent with the quiet achievements of DeLillo's fiction of the young millennium. One might imagine the two previous novels—one about a woman who learns to cope with grief through art, the other about an angry, defeated man—as the outer panels of a polyptych, or multipanel set of paintings. (Peter Boxall briefly entertains a relationship between those two works when he writes that "it may be that *The Body Artist,* in its monkish, rural retreat, makes a strong contrast to *Cosmopolis,* set as the latter is in the buzz of a futuristic city.")[23] Following this line of thought, the outer panels formed by the two previous novels are hinged together and closed like doors. Opening them reveals the panels of a third, larger painting to the viewer. In this case we might regard *Falling Man,* in which a woman and man contend with the consequence of the attack, as the center panel of the first decade of DeLillo's twenty-first-century career.

Falling Man

Announcing a novel, whereby the first words precipitate a sort of narrative chain reaction that carries through the work, has long been praised as a trademark of DeLillo's fiction. His novels begin with sharp, memorable sentences arranged in carefully tailored narrative patterns. In cases such as *Mao II* (1991) and the more recent *Point Omega* (2010), the novels' first sections are titled so as to distinguish them as distinct parts of the work. (In those two novels, the section titles are "At Yankee Stadium" and "Anonymity," respectively.) These sections are often isolated for praise, a critical habit that extends also to individual sentences. (One reviewer of *Underworld* began the essay with the memorable line "Don DeLillo is now the best writer of sentences in America.")[24] As I noted in the previous section, reviewers such as Kakutani, who invokes the "Prologue" to *Underworld* as a standard for evaluation of DeLillo in her review of *Falling Man,* and O'Hara, who judges *Falling Man* by the "magic" of its sentences, are the rule. What is lost in this praise for the celebrated beginnings of DeLillo's books is how the narration of his novels depends also upon the careful selection and placement of individual words and parts of speech, a matter whose import I hope to have explained with respect to his recent writings. This is not a way of splitting additional hairs; rather, it indicates a relationship between part and whole that DeLillo recalibrates in his late fiction.

How then might we understand these celebrated sections—as distinct sections of a novel or as integral to its entirety? As noted in the previous chapter, DeLillo regards some of them as dispensable (citing the opening of *The Names* as an example). Any answer we offer to the question will find at least one exception in DeLillo's actual works. I tend to the latter view insofar as the later novels sustain the initial arrangement of words in such a way that they accumulate and acquire density over the novel's course. In this view, we might usefully divide the narration of DeLillo's twentieth-century novels into two types. In the first type a narrator speaks in the first person, and a novel begins. David Bell in *Americana* and Jack Gladney in *White Noise* announce the novel, and a narrative catalysis proceeds in the form of a controlled reaction. As *Americana* begins, the reader will notice that the "shot" pans out, and the novel's narrative scope widens over the course of the story, from the cramped New York apartment, to New England, to the American Midwest, until it finally reaches the open landscapes of the Southwest at its conclusion.

The view is controlled insofar as we see what David wants us to see. First-person narration serves in this way as a framing device. As the scene widens, however, the narrator tends to diminish in stature. The same might be said for Jack Gladney's bookends to *White Noise,* where he describes the habits of two different yet related American crowds (those being the parents of college students and supermarket consumers). Not every one of DeLillo's twentieth-century novels diminishes the narrator by this expansive effect; the narrator of *The Names* (1982) begins from a removed position: "For a long time, I stayed away from the Acropolis" (3), only to become embroiled by virtue of increased proximity to the novel's plot.

In the second type, there is what appears to be third-person narration. At first glance, it appears passive, even aloof, but over the course of the opening pages the narration will often turn to address the reader. *The Body Artist* begins with a formal detachment but exploits the ambiguity of pronouns to draw the reader into the narrative process. Take, for instance, the opening line of *Mao II* (1991): "Here they come, marching into American sunlight." The reader, confused perhaps by the adjective (what precisely might constitute "American" sunlight?) may not recognize at first how the narration speaks to an implied audience: the crowd in the stands watching another crowd, that of the wedding ritual. The narration describes how Karen Janney's father, Rodge, experiences the scene (and also later, how Karen sees it), but it is being described *to* the reader and not directly from the character's point of view. The narration provides a certain scale that is simultaneously intimate (we are addressed) and expansive (a scene is described).

Falling Man would seem to belong to this second type. It does not draw the reader in, as did *The Body Artist,* or offer the asynchronous distance of *Cosmopolis. Falling Man*'s narration begins with a combined distance and proximity, and with them the ancillary affective categories of remembrance and shock. This may have also been the goal of the narrative's design, at least in the opening pages, which again proceeds from DeLillo's elaboration of pronouns, a common technique of the novelist's previous works. And yet the opening pages of *Falling Man* suggest both a break and a continuation of his narrative style. I mean it in the sense that the chapter perfectly exemplifies DeLillo's vaunted "style" but also dulls it, as if to resist the temptation to deliver a "spectacular" opening salvo to an audience that clearly pressed him for one in reviews of his previous novel.

The novel begins: "It was not a street anymore but a world, a time and space of falling ash and near night" (3). As was the case in DeLillo's prior two books, the narrative's artistic burden is placed on the pronoun—the ambiguity of "it." To what does "it" refer? The street itself is negated in favor of abstractions: "world," "time," "space," and "near-night." Rather than focus on one, the narration elaborates the cosmological connotations of the lot over a series of conceits, the most prominent being a geological one that shapes the reader's perception of "it." Things are defined in negative terms; they are conjoined, broken apart, and rendered. *Falling Man* begins in this way, with syntactic ruptures, metaphorical dead-ends, and by a sort of shaken narrative accumulation of things, random things, as a novel of consequence. DeLillo has taken the pronominal emphasis of his recent narrative designs and exploded it on the page as if to illustrate "those things are no longer applicable to 'it.'"

A figure appears from the debris and shock. It is the silhouette of an observer who was previously implied. Now the pronouns assume another function—that of gathering a point of view from the cosmic wreck. We note "he," "him," and "his," the masculine pronouns assuming a tenuous coherence as the scene unfolds. Three quarters of the way through the chapter, the reader finds this passage: "He heard the sound of the second fall, or felt it in the trembling air, the north tower coming down, a soft awe of voices in the distance. That was him coming down, the north tower" (5). At this point, the reader infers that "he" had previously left a different tower, but the metaphorical conjunction between "him" and "the north tower," which thereby links a person with an object of incomparable magnitude, comes apart both literally and figuratively at the moment it is suggested. Clearly, *Falling Man* is *not* a novel without philosophical ambitions, ambitions that are evident in these poetic ruptures between words and the things to which they refer. Readers who clamored for spectacle were sure to be disappointed by the somber, fractured lines of the novel's first pages. Certainly, one can ignore "it" in the search for other things. For instance, one can judge *Falling Man* for the philosophical or political assumptions of its premise, which posits a "world" in which language, in a state of shock, has temporarily lost its coherence, but one cannot dispute the artful craftsmanship with which DeLillo has designed the narration of the book's opening chapter, as if to refuse expectation.

Diffidence, one might call it, but it is diffidence with respect to the signature "first lines" of DeLillo's own career as well as audience expectations. If one looks closely, the components of that heralded style are strategically placed in the ruin of the scene. There is the implied catastrophe, a world historical event aspiring to genocide. There is a character emerging from shock. The prose is ironically terse and observant to detail. Evidence of global capitalism (one might regard it as the destruction of the office files and furniture that attracted David's attention in the opening chapters of *Americana*) litters the air and ground. The narration notes "the tai chi group from the park nearby" (4), frozen in their stances, a scene reminiscent of a similar moment in DeLillo's *Running Dog* (1978) and also a reminder of his interest in Asian religions and particularly variants of Buddhism that stress physical discipline. There is a conceit that connects "him" to the tower, "the world," and a cosmology, but it is in collapse (as opposed to the pervasive, amorphous figure of "white noise"). "It" is coming done (in slow-motion, of course).

The process will continue over the course of the novel with respect to the figure of the initial observer who emerges from the event (but never quite from his shock). "His" pronouns will slowly assume identity, history, and community, even the specificity of a name (Keith) over the following chapters. But *Falling Man* will also move in the opposite direction, developing a counterpoint to "it," a pronoun against whose lack of clarity a new protagonist appears in increasingly sharper and antithetical relief: Lianne.

It is useful to regard *Falling Man* as a mirror image of *White Noise* (1985). Like that earlier novel, *Falling Man* is a melodrama about a postnuclear family set in the aftermath of a disaster. In the latter novel's case, the principal characters are Keith Neudecker and Lianne. (Some commentators refer to Lianne as Lianne Neudecker, but she is never named as such in the novel; Keith and Lianne are legally separated, and Lianne most often identifies with the "Glenn," her father's name.) Previously married, Keith and Lianne were legally separated (not divorced) and living apart prior to the period in which the novel is set. They are parents to a son named Justin, who lives with Lianne on the Upper West Side of Manhattan. (Keith lived in an apartment across from the World Trade Center, at the southern end of the island.) Keith is the observer of events in the opening chapter, although he is not named until the novel's second chapter, as if the shock of survival had estranged him from his own name. Thereafter he inhabits the name with discomfort, only to recede again into anonymity and the amnesiac spaces of the American Southwest.

Lianne offers a far different trajectory. In *White Noise,* for example, the extended families of Jack and Babette had no significant presence of which to speak. (Only Babette's father briefly appears in the book.) Keith's family is also largely absent. His father visits from Western Pennsylvania, three years after the novel begins, but never appears in a scene, remaining instead in a nearby room of the apartment. Lianne's father and mother have a significant presence in the novel. Her mother, Nina, is a retired art historian who lives nearby. Lianne's father, Jack, committed suicide years before, at the onset of symptoms of Alzheimer's disease. Lianne believes he did so because he wanted to spare her his inability to recognize her. While Jack's influence is significant in Lianne's life—she runs a writing workshop for persons with Alzheimer's disease, for example—Nina has a more powerful presence in the novel. She and her lover, Martin, often host Lianne and Justin. They discuss art, politics, and history, and their conversations often ruminate on life after "it." Just as significant is the fact of these conversations. As opposed to the postgenealogical characters of *White Noise,* Lianne's interactions with her family sustain multigenerational narrative modes for much of the novel. If the disruption of the opening pages is a geological surface movement, then these multigenerational narratives function as a planetary core, exerting a centripetal, stabilizing energy for Lianne.

The plot of the novel may be summarized as follows: Lianne and Keith attempt to reconcile their marriage after "it." As Linda S. Kaufmann has noted in an excellent review of the novel's narrative of their broken family, the two characters "resume a semblance of family life, though the conflicts that drove them to part remain unresolved."[25] In this context Keith, his downtown apartment destroyed, returns to live with Lianne and Justin. Keith's wrist is injured during his flight, and he must rehabilitate it with a regimen that recurs throughout the novel. Lianne proceeds with her own work as a leader of the writing group and also as a freelance editor. In the weeks that follow the novel's opening scene, Keith slightly recovers from the initial shock by finding consolation with another survivor of the attack, an African American woman named Florence, and the two commence a brief romantic affair. Both together and as separate individuals, Lianne and Keith contend with an array of reactions and emotions, many of them conflicted, after the attack. Following the reconciliation, Keith begins to drift away from New York City, living between Nevada, where he gambles, and New York City, while increasingly favoring the former place. Lianne remains in New York City with Justin.

Spread over fourteen somber chapters, this family melodrama constitutes *Falling Man*'s primary terrain. Many of DeLillo's signature narrative techniques appear throughout the novel, but as with the case of the family melodrama, they are often stripped of any comic or absurdist pretense. Take "the crowd," for instance. In the opening lines of previous novels such as *Mao II* and *Underworld,* for instance, crowds are afforded an extraordinary complexity in a manner that suggests a sentience independent of the individuals who compose them. Those crowds express comedy and terror, become locations of intrigue and surprise, and function as engines of art and history. By contrast, there is a scene in *Falling Man* in which Keith listens to Florence describe the masses of employees escaping the building prior to its collapse. Florence recounts her descent, the same stairwell, and the details of the crowd; Keith recognizes fragments of his own escape in her words. He returns to the memory through her eyes, but try as he might, he cannot see himself among the fleeing workers. Although it would seem to bring them together, the mass experience ultimately divides them. In the end, they are linked only by Florence's briefcase, which Keith absentmindedly picked up as he fled and which he has since returned to her. For Keith, crowds have lost their wondrous vitality and their capacity to function as the imaginative witnesses (and substitutes) to historical events. Crowds have fallen silent.

Imagination, memory, and the ability to react with either thought or affect are instead reserved for Lianne, who recovers those abilities after an initial period of shock. In describing a scene from the book at the beginning of this chapter, I noted how Lianne dwells upon a still-life painting, bringing it to life, as it were, through the ensuing conversation between her, Nina, and Martin. In a recent essay, Julia Apitzsch has noted that DeLillo replaced the "media images that constitute our experience of the event" with figural and performance art, the still-life painting of the scene in question representing the former group.[26] Whereas the crowd no longer speaks to Keith, Lianne listens to art. Here is the response and solution—complicated, introspective, and thoughtful—to the horrific shock that opens the novel. Whereas Keith is locked into his subjective view of the event, Lianne escapes that subjectivity by virtue of an exchange. Her relationship to objects is an imaginative and critical one. In the end, as Apitzsch is correct to note, Lianne and her mother, Nina, must return the still-life paintings to Martin because "they now link his shady past to the present terrorist activities in ways that cast a new light on everything."[27] Nina returns to visit the paintings when they are exhibited in a New York gallery.

The function of art in *Falling Man* is not limited to what Apitzsch describes as Lianne's "ekphrastic" perspective, which transforms the novel into a still life of sorts. There is a second art form with which to contend in the novel: photography. It is embodied by the infamous and iconic "Falling Man" photograph to which the novel alludes in an extraordinarily difficult manner, not by reproducing it, as it were, but by creating a fictional character who recreates the photograph as a public performance wherein he suspends himself from buildings. Whereas the still-life painting invites Lianne to pensive reflection, Falling Man provokes anger and shock. The two figures mark key points along the broad affective spectrum whereby Lianne responds to and processes the tragic day. DeLillo's fictional re-creation of the photograph in art may be said to intervene in and complicate a comparable public catharsis that generated controversy and debate around the relationship between art and terror. As John N. Duvall has noted, "Falling Man is a terrorist of perception."[28] Duvall proceeds to note how "a number of visual artists tried to represent the particular horror evoked by those who jumped from the towers rather than burn to death. The contemporary response to these artistic meditations was quite negative."[29]

Apitzsch describes the photograph's function as follows: "The fictitious Falling Man [in DeLillo's novel] echoes the infamous photograph taken by Richard Drew of one victim jumping out of a tower window. The photo was printed on page 7 of the *New York Times* and reprinted by various other newspapers. It became known under the title 'Falling Man,' and it created a scandal among people because of its alleged sensationalist exploitation of terror."[30] The photograph itself was taken from the street level in lower Manhattan, and it captures a person descending—it is not clear whether the figure jumped or fell. The photograph was later the subject of a September 2003 article written by Tom Junod for *Esquire* magazine. (A follow-up to the original article was published in that same magazine in 2011.) A documentary film, loosely based upon Junod's original *Esquire* article, was released in 2006. With respect to the photograph itself, it is difficult to resist a critique of its "iconic" status, and one must acknowledge the widespread dispute that surrounded the photo. Does the photo violate the terrible privacy of a dying man's desperate choice? Is it exploitation of the event, a fragment of a spectacle published only to sell newspapers and thereby profit from tragedy? Or is the very fact of its publication an assertion of unwavering commitment, on behalf of a free press, to inform the public? Each of these questions assumes a motive of design or an intention prior to the fact of publication.

All of these precedents would seem to guarantee a causal relationship between the image and DeLillo's novel; yet DeLillo has insisted in interviews that his novel was not "inspired" by the photograph in any way. One cannot assume DeLillo's ignorance of the matter, given the role of the media in his fiction, his predisposition to newsprint, the resemblance between the photograph and Falling Man's poses, and so forth. With respect to the novel itself, the questions raised about the photograph's possible role as source material must shift into a different frame. In the first place, the novel does not reproduce the photograph in any visual form. The novel alludes to Drew's photograph at several points. At one point in the closing chapter, Keith, the man who "was . . . coming down, the north tower" (5) in the opening pages, may catch a glimpse at the field of his vision of a person falling from one of the tower's upper floors in the minutes after "it" occurs. In these instances, the premise and moment of Drew's photograph occupies a rhetorical space at the edge of the novel, a space from which it is never entirely assimilated into the work.

In the second place, the novel portrays instead a man named David Janiak, a parachutist, who calls himself Falling Man and suspends himself from tall structures in New York City. Readers are never privy to objective descriptions of the figure; rather, we only know of David through Lianne's reactions to him, either in person or in news reports. Lianne reacts in critical fashion during one of the novel's more complex scenes. The novel's ninth chapter shows Lianne walking across Manhattan's Upper East Side as she seeks a patient who has gone missing from the writing workshop that Lianne conducts every week. She passes housing projects and notices children at play. A hush descends, and concerned faces appear in the windows of the buildings. They are all looking in Lianne's direction, but not directly at her person. She looks up and sees Falling Man waiting in a position above and to the side of a subway track that emerges from a nearby tunnel. Lianne turns her attention to the spectators, then back to the waiting David Janiak. She realizes the spectacle is not meant for the residents but for the commuters of a train that is speeding through the tunnel. Janiak leaps, and Lianne now watches the shocked commuters who react to his three-dimensional replication of the photograph. The aesthetic action is comparable to when Lianne animates the still life in her mother's apartment, the difference being that Janiak's re-creation of the photograph is public, spectacular, and provocative. The complex narration of the scene, in which Lianne observes two sets of observers as well as Janiak (all of whom do not seem to note her presence), is as carefully orchestrated as any narrative sequence in DeLillo's prose. The effect, however, is again different: Lianne recoils before the scene, which comprises both the spectators and Falling Man (as opposed to Janiak alone). We know that her point of view is unique, but we do not know what shocks her. Is it the physical risk of Janiak's leap from his perch? The commuters' faces twisting into frightened expressions? The neighborhood's apprehensive residents whom Janiak and the commuters, but not Lianne, appear to ignore?

There is also the sudden nature of Falling Man's performance to consider, the strategy of which is significant in its own right. Linda Kauffmann describes Janiak as an artist who "purposefully avoids the celebrity that most of the culture craves. Each jump is spontaneous, so the media cannot record it. He depends on the element of surprise, and refuses to explain his actions, motives, or intentions."[31] Kauffmann's published essays on DeLillo's *Falling Man* are particularly insightful, and they merit special consideration. In the article just cited, she ultimately argues that both Falling Man (Janiak) and the novel's use of the genre of the family melodrama resist assimilation: "*Falling Man* defies tidy categorization of every sort, including those related to sexual politics."[32] Furthermore, as Apitzsch notes, DeLillo insists upon replacing media spectacle with art in the novel. Regarded together, these are the means and the end of *Falling Man.* Art is the means by which Lianne "tries valiantly to work through the trauma [of 'it']," as Kauffmann writes in another essay.[33] In this view of DeLillo's *Falling Man,* Lianne attains a status comparable to that of Lauren Hartke in *The Body Artist* or Bill Gray in *Mao II* insofar as each exhibits a fierce and altruistic determination to survive in, through, and by thoughtful and critical response to works of art.

There remains, however, one aspect of DeLillo's novel that has not been commented on at any length, although certain critics have alluded to it. I have drawn attention to the episodic structure of DeLillo's novels. That structure includes the extensive use of separately labeled interchapters that interrupt the flow of chapters, or even chapters that function as counter-narratives to the central plot, as was the case in the "diary" chapters of *Cosmopolis,* and also DeLillo's dust jackets, or photographs reproduced between parts of a novel (as in *Mao II*). *Falling Man* adopts a similar pattern in that its fourteen chapters are divided into three parts, respectively titled "Bill Lawton," "Ernst Hechinger," and "David Janiak." The numbered chapters within each part are devoted to Keith and Lianne, but each of the three parts concludes with a separately titled interchapter. The interchapters are labeled "Marienstrasse," "In Nokomis," and "In The Hudson Corridor," the last of which ends *Falling Man.*

The three interchapters appear to be loosely based upon the account of the terrorist hijackers described by *The 9/11 Commission Report* (2004). The protagonist of these interchapters is a fictional character, a young Arab man named Hammad. He is a hijacker trained to subdue passengers while other terrorists take over airplane control systems. Although there was no hijacker by that name on any of the four hijacked planes—Hammad is depicted as being on the plane that strikes the south tower of the World Trade Center, the first of the four planes to crash—his story follows the exact details of that plot. (One of the other terrorists who actually hijacked the planes is named in DeLillo's novel.) The difference is that DeLillo's narration strips away the sociopolitical commentary that typifies the official documents, revealing in its place a bare narrative of indoctrination.

Hammad's story begins in Hamburg, Germany, where he studies engineering and falls in love with a Muslim woman. He lives in a crowded apartment with other members of the cell. It proceeds in the second interchapter to flight training in Florida, where the pilots are separated from the other hijackers, who would murder the crew and contain the passengers during the flight. In the first two interchapters, Hammad is divided between skepticism and loyalty to his peers. The character development is reminiscent of Karen Janney's in *Mao II.* Skepticism modulates the development of both characters: for Karen it is manifest in the form of family memory; for Hammad it appears in the form of a girlfriend named Leyla. Karen's doubts eventually lead her away from the cult, however, whereas Hammad's doubts accede to complete zealotry. There is a second difference: in *Mao II* the reader is not privy to Karen's induction into the cult. There is instead the opening scene that describes her near-complete devotion, the flashback (told by Scott) of her incomplete deprogramming and escape, and finally, from Karen's point of view, her mystical, phantasmagoric vision of New York City. In *Falling Man* the narration surveys the social process of Hammad's radicalization. The process combines a psychological group dynamic with the presence of a tyrannical figure. In the former case, the group punishes bad Muslims, and Hammad must beat a man; in the latter case, Hammad is shown to wither before the paranoid exhortations of Amir, the cell's leader. (Amir is part of the full name of one of the actual 9/11 terrorists.) The cell's dynamic also includes a regimen of physical discipline. In every case—doctrine, exercise, or violence—preparation for the attack involves adherence to routine. The "Marienstrasse" chapter is terse, with sparse sentences that convey an atmosphere of ascetic preparation. In this way DeLillo depicts fanaticism as moving away from self-realization. As opposed to bildungsroman, Hammad's story describes a "de-selfing"—an erasure of his earthly attachments to things, ambitions, family, loved ones, and friends—to all but his fellow conspirators.

The critical response to Hammad has been complex. In its most heated moments, critics have ventured fierce accusations regarding the limits of DeLillo's imagination. For instance, Sascha Pöhlmann has argued that *Falling Man* "does not succeed in imagining the terrorist as anything other than an Orientalist construction of an Islamist terrorist."[34] In one of three essays she has published on *Falling Man,* Linda S. Kauffman has regarded Hammad instead as a "three-dimensional" character whose religious "doubt" makes him "particularly memorable."[35] While Pöhlmann regards the novel within a broad ideological framework and Kauffman considers it in light of the novelist's post-9/11 writings, Paula Martín Salván's has placed Hammad along the ascetic figures that appear throughout DeLillo's novels, these generally being characters who are "involved in a search for some form of transcendence."[36] Salván makes a number of insightful arguments in her essay (correctly noting, for example, the qualitative disparity between *Falling Man* and John Updike's ill-conceived 2006 novel *The Terrorist*). The most relevant to our present discussion of the novel's episodic structure is her argument regarding the relationship between the brief, epigrammatic prose style and the novel's other characters, when she writes that "the dissolution of writing itself at the end of an ascetic process is a device DeLillo uses elsewhere in *Falling Man.*"[37] In Salván's view, the asceticism extends to Keith and later encompasses a more general function of the novel that posits "storytelling as a means to confront terrorism."[38] This view is a reasonable one, even as it would seem to confirm Pöhlmann's accusation regarding the novel's ideological orientation vis-à-vis the privileged role of art. But Salván's is also incomplete insofar as it does not contend with the narration of the novel's final interchapter, "In the Hudson Corridor," and what that narration implies with respect to the novel's design.

In the later chapters of *Falling Man,* Lianne and Keith begin to separate once again. At the same time a mirroring effect embedded in the narration reflects the figural movements of Lianne, Keith, and Hammad. In chapter 14 Keith returns to gambling in Las Vegas. He continues his routines, his wrist-rehabilitation exercises of flexing and stretching (scenes that illustrate Salván's point regarding asceticism). Lianne turns instead to community, to family, and to the Catholic Mass. Unlike that of the male characters, Lianne's routine is not self-annihilating, nor is it a prop that merely juxtaposes Keith and Hammad, who are drawing closer even as the novel appears to move away from "it" in time. As noted above, the third and final interchapter, entitled "In The Hudson Corridor," closes *Falling Man.* When the hijacked airplane hits the south tower, a sentence that begins with Hammad ends with Keith: "A bottle fell off the counter in the galley, on the other side of the aisle, he watched it roll this way and that, a water bottle, empty, making an arc one way and rolling back the other, and he watched it spin more quickly and then skitter across the floor an instant before the aircraft struck the tower, heat, then fuel, then fire, and a blast wave passed through the structure that sent Keith Neudecker out of his chair and into a wall" (239).

It is notable that DeLillo does not use pronouns here to confuse the two men (as the reader is confused with Lauren in *The Body Artist,* for example). Hammad has long since become depersonalized, the pronoun "he" working as a substitute for the proper noun in the final interchapter. Keith is named in the sentence, however, but if the reader recalls Keith was also reduced to a pronoun in the novel's opening chapter, a shocked nominal status from which he slowly emerges, but never entirely, over the course of the book, his name becomes something arbitrary, even uncomfortable along the way.

Falling Man's cyclical structure would appear to suggest a condemnation of violent socioreligious conflict, whose modern ethos and causes, it suggests, are embodied in the masculine characters of Hammad, Keith, and Martin. From the opening narration in which Keith materializes only to come apart once again over the novel's course (only to return to the traumatic moment), it would suggest a bleak view of history to which Lianne is the counterweight. The characters are never idealized or flattened to thin ideas: Hammad doubts his devotion, Keith tries to regain integrity but fails, Lianne's anger upsets her attempts to comprehend the motives for the attack, and so forth through

Florence and Nina, Martin and Justin. Is it true, given the forms of violence, not all of them physical, that characters commit against one another, that *Falling Man* is designed in some way to heal the "trauma" of the event? Can we return to a prior state, the novel seems to ask, as we continue to behave in this manner? If we raise these questions, we risk reducing the novel to a morality play, a work whose didactic impulse is extracted from the substance of its design. The design itself, from the claustrophobia of its opening pages through the violent momentum of its alternating chapters, interchapters, and parts, suggests a novel that regards its own aesthetic design as necessary and suspicious, as well as intrusive, violent, and conclusive (similar, in this way, to how Lianne regards David Janiak), yet also introspective, critical, and expansive (similar, in this way, to Lianne's relationship to her mother's collection of still-life paintings). The pattern is consistent with the narrative experiments of DeLillo's works of the new century. *The Body Artist* drew the reader into the peculiar linguistic temporalities of its syntax, and *Cosmopolis* proposed that markets effected technological and cognitive ruptures in the narrative perception of time. In *Falling Man* narrative time is instead cyclical, and violently so: characters and readers are placed in a position to simultaneously recoil from historical memory and experience. *Falling Man* does not convey those cycles as a media loop by which the repetition of an image becomes nauseatingly common, nor does it advocate a specific historical model (for example, the cyclical model of history proposed by Giambattista Vico). Unlike its predecessors, *Falling Man* dramatizes time as traveling along individual and communal currents and countercurrents. It does not represent historical time but rather rival and turbulent perceptions of it, those perceptions that the novel correctly claims to belong to the flow of aesthetic experience (as opposed to those of mediated commercial time or that of rationalized, historical time). These are the wells from which spring revolutions of violence as well as virtue.

As noted earlier, the critical reception of *Falling Man* has been mixed. When regarded within that strange "genre" of post-9/11 fiction, it certainly does not resemble the mood or design of other books that are included in the lot, most of which were being written more or less at the same time that DeLillo composed *Falling Man*. Absent are the relativist fantasies of Updike's *The Terrorist,* a book about a radicalized Arab American teenager whom the novelist admitted to researching while being escorted by car through Paterson, New Jersey (presumably because it was documented that some of the 9/11 hijackers passed through that city's large Arab American community prior to the attack). If *Falling Man* is to be compared to other treatments of "it," a pronoun the novel uses to indicate amorphous shock as well an event that was its cause, it should also be noted that DeLillo does not venture into the weak comparative historicity of a novel such as Jonathan Safran Foer's *Extremely Loud and Incredibly Close* (2006), which lightly equates 9/11 to the Allied firebombing of Dresden, Germany, during World War II (the latter having been the occasion for Vonnegut's *Slaughterhouse-Five*). And with respect to other prior works of American literature, *Falling Man* did not attempt to elaborate any classic figure of American literary rhetoric (as did Joseph O'Neill in returning to Whitman's *Leaves of Grass* in his 2008 novel *Netherland*). In their essays Pöhlmann and Salván express criticism and articulate reservations about the status of DeLillo's novel vis-à-vis these other works (they do not mention O'Neill's novel, however), and other critics have attempted to define the relationship of DeLillo's novel to the event along other trajectories.[39] One could draw any number of comparisons, perhaps at the risk of unfairly implying that the novels in question were written in a vacuum or in some implicit dialogue with one another. Regardless, the novels enter into a context, one that precedes the event in question and continues after the fact; and they enter a market in which readers flocked to bookstores to purchase books that might explain the event either directly (one recalls *The 9/11 Commission Report,* a best-selling government document) or indirectly (sales of spiritual and religious writings likewise increased after the attack). *Falling Man* can fairly be said to avoid comparison to the other novels that were published in the first decade after "it" happened. In doing so, one risks making it exceptional on the one hand, with all the cultural chauvinism that term entails, or appealing ad hominem on the other to DeLillo's own stated preoccupation that the novel today functions at the edges of culture, its presence diminished by terror and the media.

If a fair comparison can be made, one might note that the novel affirms the latter option in that *Falling Man* is consistent with DeLillo's refusal to write in such a way that would merely "entertain" a reader. Referring to DeLillo's post-9/11 essay "In the Ruins of the Future," Sascha Pöhlmann notes that "while the nation clamored for answers [following 9/11], DeLillo resolved instead to ask more questions."[40] The essay's maneuver is typical of the inconclusive manner of his previous novels. As noted earlier, elements of *Falling Man* (Keith's drifting into the Southwest, for example, or his cinematic alternate take on the scene when he returns to his ruined apartment) follow long-established habits in DeLillo's fiction (even if their use is subdued). This was perhaps the mistake that many readers and critics made when reviewing the book: they expected it to conform to an earlier pattern by which DeLillo would again summon the spectacular metafictions of his mid-career success and that he would direct that arsenal against the attack so as to expose the media, terrorists, plots, and jargon that largely shaped our response to it.

Critics nearly demanded it: after all, DeLillo was a prophet, and eventually the prophet must speak. And speak he did, as *Falling Man* delivers what appears to be a rebuke to that section of his audience who demanded of the oracle that expectations be met.

Falling Man contains a sequence in which Lianne meets with an editor, Carol Shoup. Carol works for a publishing firm that occasionally hires Lianne to edit books as an independent contractor, thereby outsourcing work to her, as it were. Carol offers Lianne to edit the manuscript of a nonfiction book, which is implied to be an academic study that "seems to predict what happened" (138). Returning to the loaded pronoun of the novel's opening line, DeLillo has Carol further describe a "book that is so enormously immersed, going back on it, leading up to it. And a book that's so demanding, so incredibly tedious" (138). Lianne responds wryly by repeating Carol's phrase "seems to predict" in the dialogue they exchange during their meeting. Here is metafiction, but not of the kind that DeLillo's reviewers requested.

DeLillo may have directed the book offer scene against critics, but he may have also addressed the publishing industry in that moment. It is a recurrent habit: Fenig the genre writer rails against it in *Great Jones Street* (1973), and three separate characters—Bill, Scott, and Charles (an important editor at a major publishing firm) all offer their largely negative views on it in *Mao II*. Lianne provides a curt reply to the industry's rush to publish books that would not have otherwise been published had the attack not occurred. (As Carol notes in the scene, the manuscript in question circulated among publishers prior to the attack but was rejected at that time.)

Broadening the view of the implied criticism of the industry, one returns to Julia Apitzsch's argument that *Falling Man* avoids long discursions on the mass media (discursions for which DeLillo had become famous in other novels, such as *White Noise* and *Mao II*). Is it fair to suggest that DeLillo's novel fulminates in some way against the media and its technicians, the editors, producers, and pundits who, churned by vengeance-minded propaganda, plunged the republic into a new type of bloodlust? Perhaps. *Falling Man* would appear in this view a novel that asserts the institution of literary narrative against "it," the latter being an expansive and terrible thing that would seem to be slouching towards Bethlehem through the sum of our actions. In that position *Falling Man* does not ask, "How are you complicit?" but rather, "What do I expect from this novel, or any novel or other work of art?" If we seek familiarity and its distracting comforts, delusion is sure to follow. To ask such a question as thousands die, tens of thousands and millions in the years that follow, continuously and without end in sight, while corrupt and cynical bureaucrats and ideological technicians spout clichés even as they transform war into a more sophisticated form of capitalism or make bedfellows with the very prophets that DeLillo depicts in his fiction (Linda Kauffman has noted the 2004 ceremony in the U.S. Capitol building honoring the Reverend Moon, one of the demagogues portrayed in *Mao II*), would furthermore seem a matter of minor and privileged concern in light of the blood spilled since a fanatical gang of murderers visited "it" upon New York.[41] "It" is a day, whereby time has become a figure of some intractable space, and a day that does not end in DeLillo's novel.

The early pages of this book referred to Edward W. Said's writings on "late style." Said describes three phases—early, middle, and late—in the history of the modern novel. He assigns them also to the shape of writer's careers. He notes that in late style a "special maturity" becomes manifest.[42] It can take one of two forms. In the case of the composer Giuseppe Verdi, the late works "exude not so much a spirit of wise resignation as a renewed, almost youthful energy that attests to an apotheosis of artistic creativity and power." Other artists, such as the novelist Giuseppe Tomasi di Lampedusa, exemplify another lateness, one that "involves a nonharmonious, nonserene tension, and above all, a sort of deliberately unproductive productiveness going against."[43] I have found it useful to regard DeLillo's later works in this way, with some distinctions. *Falling Man* and *Point Omega* come closest to the mood of Lampedusa wherein older orders persist to complicate the present time. In both cases a quasi-imperial American conservatism provides the example, with Richard Elster, the former Vietnam-era military official of *Point Omega,* being representative. (Linda Wagner Martin aptly described the latter novel as effectively offering "depletion.")[44] By contrast, the technical innovations of *The Body Artist* and *Cosmopolis* approximate the youthful energies of the late Verdi. What unites them above these distinctions is another impulse, one that might be described as DeLillo's stubborn refusal to admit the present time as the only available path the future might take. In this turbulent temporal frame, Eric Packer must be a victim of his own disgust for obsolescence because he would otherwise represent the future, Lianne must refuse to accept the terrorist's terms because she would otherwise abandon what she imagines the future might be, and Lauren must continue refining her performance by working into the future through but also against the drag of memory. The same may be said for the later short stories, even the somewhat lighthearted "Hammer and Sickle," wherein DeLillo's prose does not delight in the absurd so much as relinquish it to another generation, to youth, and the protagonist seeks instead a resolve that will allow him to face the future, even if in finding that resolve he must once again break the law.

In the end, *Falling Man* does not portray novelists and terrorists but survivors and suicides. The resulting perspective avoids the psychedelic tumult of Karen Janney's synesthesia in *Mao II,* replacing it instead with the quiet manner in which Lianne regards a still life. It is not an excited view that suggests youthful provocation or the historical force of a later confidence. As the protagonists of the three novels near or begin middle age, we feel that DeLillo writes to remind us that a novel is not made from the sentiments it provides to its audience but from the vulnerable possibility of sentiments which that audience has not yet recognized.

CHAPTER 5

With, to, and against the Novel

The Short Stories

Don DeLillo is known primarily for his literary novels despite his significant contributions to other literary modes. This is in part because until recently DeLillo's stories were published in many small periodicals and magazines. Scattered over a number of decades, some proved hard to find, thereby presenting a problem of access to the reader and critic (some of his early fiction remains uncollected). Access is not the only reason for why DeLillo's short fiction has not been widely discussed; another factor is DeLillo's habit of considering the short story as a distinct mode requiring a writer to foreground different elements of the craft. To complicate this aesthetic distinction, DeLillo has nonetheless revised stories and then integrated them into longer works. Yet, while DeLillo's novels have attracted a great deal of critical attention, very little has been written about his work as a short story writer.

In "The Angel Esmeralda," a DeLillo short story that originally appeared in *Esquire* (1994) and then in a 2011 collection bearing the same title as the story (page citations are from that volume), an elderly nun named Edgar rises from bed and prepares for her day. She washes and prays. She dons her vestments, which the younger nuns do not wear. Edgar and her sisters leave their church in the New York borough of the Bronx to pick up and then deliver food to the poor. A priest asks the sisters to look for a young girl whom he believes to be homeless and living in the empty buildings of the South Bronx neighborhood known in the story as "the Bird," a nickname given to it by the local police. Edgar notes the request. Before the nuns distribute food to the poor, Edgar dons a pair of latex gloves.

Edgar is observant, even severely so. She notices every detail of a person's speech and gesture, and every smell and every stone of her surroundings. It is a habit reinforced by her fear of germs and her aversion to contact. (She no longer disciplines students by force but persuades herself that this is because of changes in the community's demographics, not her avoidance of physical contact.) Edgar's reputation among the younger sisters is that of a strict nun. It is one that she does not refuse, even if it is no longer true. Edgar's scrupulous powers of observation have, however, complicated her faith, so much so that doubt has entered her heart. Edgar does not retire from the church, and the younger nuns do not understand her desire to stay. After the nuns distribute the food, they are caught in traffic. An irascible younger nun named Gracie spots the young girl after whom the priest inquired and chases her. Gracie returns alone. Several weeks later, the nuns learn that Esmeralda, the young girl of the empty lots, was raped and murdered.

In the story's final pages, the nuns receive rumor of a miracle in the community. Crowds are gathering to see it. Gracie admonishes Edgar and a nun named Jan, both of whom express a desire to witness the phenomenon in question, and depart to see it with their own eyes. The assembled crowd parts for the two sisters. A train passes, shining a light on a large billboard. A face appears from the surface of the sign; it is the face of the murdered girl, Esmeralda. Edgar sees it, too. A wave of joyous recognition breaks over the crowd. When the crowd hugs Edgar, she forgets to recoil. DeLillo writes, "She embraced Sister Jan. They shook hands, pumped hands with the great-bodied women who rolled their eyes to heaven. The women did great two-handed pump shakes, fabricated words jumping out of their mouths, trance utterance, Edgar thought—they're singing of things outside the known deliriums. She thumped a man's chest with her fists" (99). The narration, which has been as meticulous as Edgar in noting her aversion to physical contact and the preparations she makes to avoid it, does not note at any point that Edgar is not wearing her gloves. In the final lines, the narration repeats much of the opening scene. But when Edgar rises from bed and prays this morning the long opening discourse on cleansing that first indicates Edgar's doubt is replaced with a line of prayer.

DeLillo's short stories pose particular challenges to readers of his novels. Whereas the novel invites commodification—as book, as film, as literary institution, and the privileged object of literary canons—the story is an ephemeral commodity. In DeLillo's novels our cultural amnesia is substantiated, its historical development spelled out and dramatized in affective modes of stunned apprehension. The novels are systems that disrupt other systems. His short stories are instead objects of art that move in another direction, away from systemic modes of narrative organization, taking the reliquary form of myth. In "Creation" (1979) two characters, a man and woman, are stranded on a Caribbean Island by ineffective bureaucracies, playing out Edenic desires. In "The Ivory Acrobat" (1988) a young teacher cannot help but think that the Hellenic gods persist; she survives by meditating on the broken ivory statue of a woman performing a somersault over the horns of a charging bull. While in his novels history operates according to chance and probability, DeLillo instead favors the fateful mood of the epic fragment in his short stories. Atmospheric subjectivity displaces the impossible objectivity of the novel's panoramic scope; whereas glossolalia and aphasia gesture in the novels toward the confusion of capital and culture, the "trance utterances" that appear in "The Angel Esmeralda" occur as forms of mythic vocalization. The effect may be similar to what Walt Whitman described in "Song of Myself" as "Nature without check with original energy." In these ways and others, DeLillo's short stories do not provide the historical sequences and contexts offered by his novels. This is not to suggest that the short stories operate "outside" history but that their relationship to historical time—an element so integral to DeLillo's novels—travels along other, more ephemeral trajectories. This is only partly due to their transient commodity form.

In a well-written discussion of the modern short story's treatment of time, Michael Trussler remarked that "the short story pertains to the complexity of negotiating temporal experience through narrative."[1] As opposed to the novel, which organizes time along a spectrum (most often the sequential one of characters' lives), Trussler writes, "Many short stories depict situations where characters are perplexed by a given set of circumstances."[2] In the case of Edgar in "The Angel Esmeralda," for instance, the possibility of religious eternity revealed to her in the final pages transforms her secular biography. Prior to revelation, she had been "suspended," to use Trussler's term, in a historical context of which she was acutely aware, yet without any figural or literal contact. In the final scene, the reader learns that she will remain in that transformed context for an additional ten years. One may regard it either as her historical debut, or her spiritual awakening, or some combination of the two, but the fact is that time begins for Edgar when the story ends. In classical myth the gods visit mortals, but the mortals do not visit Olympus.

It is important to note that in the opening paragraph of his essay, Trussler summarizes DeLillo scholar Tom LeClair's distinction between "excess" (a category of the longer novel) and "observation" (a property of the short story).[3] Trussler make his case against LeClair, Jameson, and others who Trussler believes are too hasty in their dismissal of the short story. As we shall see below, scholars of DeLillo's writings have paid little attention to his short fiction, and the scant criticism that has appeared is often consistent in that it regards the short fiction as a premise to introduce discussion of DeLillo's longer novels instead of treating it as a distinct aesthetic form in which DeLillo writes. It is tempting perhaps to consider DeLillo's literary short fiction as a minor endeavor, a miniature of the novels as opposed to a separate literary form unto itself. (I do not say critics admit this, but it is often implied in the manner in which they treat the stories.) There are, however, considerable material reasons for the lack of consideration. The first reason has to do with DeLillo's consistent but infrequent publication of short fiction (a pattern that suggests the care he takes to write it well). The second reason derives from the ephemeral format of publication. (DeLillo's stories were until recently scattered among different publications, some of them inaccessible or obscure, over a period of fifty years.) Finally, there is the relationship of his short stories to his recent fiction. While these factors, which range from the sparse critical writings to problems of physical accessibility to the work, may seem to diminish the import of his short fiction, the opposite may indeed be true insofar as readers may only now have the opportunity to begin to recognize, distinguish, and celebrate DeLillo's achievements in the art of the short story.

Don DeLillo only published short stories during the first decade of his career. He wrote and published six of them during the decade from 1960 to 1970. His first six published stories appeared in small literary journals and university-sponsored magazines of creative writing (such as the *Carolina Quarterly*). After publishing his first novel in 1971, the majority of his published short fiction consisted of excerpts or works in progress, with only four original short stories appearing between the years 1971 and 1982. (Keep in mind that he wrote six novels during that period and also his first play.) Following the publication of his first ten short stories—stories that appear as and are considered by scholars as individual works of fiction—DeLillo published an additional eight short stories between the years 1983 and 2011. All eight of those were reprinted in the aforementioned collection *The Angel Esmeralda* (2011), with the 1979 short story "Creation" added for a total of nine stories. As a result, most of the second half of DeLillo's career as a short story writer is now available to us in the printed book form as well as electronically. (Not all of DeLillo's published books are electronically available as digital downloads.) The majority of the short fiction from 1960 to 1982, consisting of nine of those first ten short stories, remains uncollected.

In addition to the rarity of their appearance (on average, one story roughly every three years), readers may also be confused by what precisely constitutes a DeLillo short story. For instance, he first published "Pafko at the Wall" in *Harper's* magazine (1992). It later appeared in revised form as the prologue to *Underworld* (1997), a chapter of sorts that sounded the keynote to that great historical romance. The *Underworld* version of the story was then reprinted in 2001 in a freestanding hardcover edition labeled a "novella." This edition has a feature not present in previous versions of the story: a reprint of the October 4, 1951, front page of the *New York Times,* which heralded the New York Giants' victory over the Brooklyn Dodgers for the National League pennant. The dust jacket also features the famous photograph of Dodgers left fielder Andy Pafko, the protagonist of the story, watching as the game-winning home run sails over the outfield wall. Is this stand-alone version a novella, as its dust jacket and title page proclaim, or a mixed-media work of literary and visual art? A reader of the 1992 version would have considered it a short story; twenty years later, the 1992 version is still a short story but one that migrated to other forms. This is often the case when DeLillo publishes short fiction in a magazine: it may be an excerpt from a work in progress, it may be an unrevised excerpt, or it may never appear in another form.[4]

At times it would seem the category of short fiction that "never appears in another form" invites a literary version of natural selection, and readers treat the short fiction as vestigial and rudimentary: something that refused to grow into something more. The habit is exemplified in John McClure's recent discussion of the final pages of *Underworld* (1997). The novel disperses over its course sections and variants of the story originally published as "The Angel Esmeralda," which was originally published in 1994 (and then "restored," as it were, to its original form in the eponymous 2011 collection of DeLillo's short fiction). Drawing upon the writings of Amy Hungerford, Mark Osteen, and other DeLillo scholars, McClure explains "the spiritual development of Sister Alma Edgar" in the novel, exploring the complicated and original views of modern Catholicism portrayed by DeLillo in his fiction.[5] McClure understands the "Sister Edgar" sections of *Underworld* in relation to DeLillo's wide-ranging interest in "ecstatic traditions" of religious worship (briefly using *Cosmopolis* as an example), and reviews the theological, historical, and narrative implications of the term "mystery." McClure's essay is a concise and insightful survey of its topic. In it he carefully expounds upon the relationship between DeLillo's biography and Catholicism; he chooses relevant, ample, and diverse examples from a range of novels; and his expert use of scholarly references confirms the work of a consummate DeLillo scholar. But it does not mention that "The Angel Esmeralda" was in fact originally published as a short story.

If one were to survey DeLillo's career as a short story writer in its entirety, however, the confusion surrounding it conceals important insights into his novels, his working habits, and also his public readings. Approaching the short fiction as a causal force of his entire career, we can begin to see its centrality to his other writings. Rather than regard it as something to be discarded or revised, we may see DeLillo's short fiction not only as the workshop in which he elaborates the narrative techniques of his novels and plays but also as a place where he creates finished products that are not meant for assembly into other forms. Consider the segmented organization of his novels. *Americana,* his first novel, is an episodic book divided into distinct parts and chapters. The novel's first chapter is similar in length and quality to the short fiction DeLillo wrote and published during the decade that preceded *Americana.* One might easily consider it a short story unto itself. In addition, longer chapters of *Americana* might stand as short novels in their own right. The novel's long sixth chapter, in which David narrates a fragmentary story of his family history and hometown, might easily have been extracted and published as a stand-alone novella (as was the case with the prologue to *Underworld*). When *Sports Illustrated* reprinted most of the long chapter at the middle of *End Zone,* DeLillo's second novel, the magazine's editors likely noted that the section could stand apart from the novel as an excellent short piece of sports fiction.

A long-standing economic model for literary publishing offers an explanation for the variety of DeLillo's publication of short fictional works. The mid-nineteenth-century advent of steam cylinder printing presses combined with higher literacy rates among American readers to create a market for short-format and serialized fiction in the periodical press. This shift prompted a split that Michael Denning describes as a "gradual but incomplete separation of the news and story function of the newspaper."[6] In that print economy, writers could sell their work to periodicals and (ideally) have the work reprinted and sold in book form (for which they would presumably be paid, though this was not always true for the later edition). It is an ingenious system: having introduced readers to excerpts or chapters in disposable newsprint, publishers could more easily persuade those same readers to purchase the collected excerpts in the more durable form of a dime novel or other printed book. In this way the serial chapters and stories functioned as a form of advertising for the fiction and its writer. By and large, the "incomplete separation of the news and story" format persists in those periodicals such as *Harper's* and *The New Yorker,* which sometimes publish DeLillo's stories and excerpts from his fiction.

I noted at the start of this chapter that the stories offer some insight into DeLillo's working habits and also into the longer fiction. I argued that the stories should be considered in and of themselves as separate works rather than as templates or drafts of the longer fiction. The fact is that DeLillo no longer writes very long novels. Consider DeLillo's most recent published work of literary fiction, *Point Omega* (2010). It is less than thirty pages longer than *Pafko at the Wall,* the 2001 reprint of the *Underworld* prologue. (This "novella" edition is available from the publisher now only in electronic form.) If we scan the past decade and a half of DeLillo's career, we see a pattern of shorter, more compact books. *The Body Artist* (2001) and *Point Omega* are nearly identical in length, and each is substantially shorter than the nine collected stories in *The Angel Esmeralda.* Indeed, the title story of that collection appeared in truncated form in the final pages of *Underworld.* (the collected volume of stories "restores" the story to the form of its original publication, as it were.) Like the prologue to *Underworld,* the two recent short novels/novellas are characterized by a density and tautness of style. One can almost imagine, regarding them in light of other examples, as excerpts taken from longer novels that do not exist. *Cosmopolis* (2003) and *Falling Man* (2007), the two longer novels of that same period, are also considerably shorter than three of the four that preceded it, those three being *White Noise, Libra,* and *Underworld.* (Comparison to the last is perhaps unfair, as it is twice the length of anything else that DeLillo has published.) The late trend in DeLillo's literary career has clearly favored the style of precise, short hits known to baseball aficionados as "small ball."

During a 1993 interview, DeLillo discussed the relationship between the opening scenes of *Mao II* and *Underworld* and the short story in the following way. Adam Begley, his interviewer, asked, "Could the set piece . . . be your alternative to the short story?" DeLillo replied, "I don't think of them that way. What attracts me to this format is its non-short-storyness, the high degree of stylization. In *Players* all the major characters in the novel appear in the prologue—embryonically, not yet named or defined. . . . This piece is the novel in miniature. It lies outside the novel. It's modular—keep it in or take it out. The mass wedding in *Mao II* is more conventional. It introduces a single major character and sets up themes and resonances. The book makes no sense without it."[7]

The economics of literary publishing, accessibility to the short stories in their periodical form, and the trend towards more compact literary forms complicate the role of short fiction in DeLillo's career. Few major authors publish short fiction with any consistency once they have achieved a certain success. As a practical matter, the explanation seems obvious: it is difficult if not impossible to earn a living on short fiction. (One might consider the plight of Fenig, the impoverished short story writer who lives above Bucky in DeLillo's *Great Jones Street,* as exemplary.) If one is to continue working with consistency and innovation in the form, it must be out of devotion to the short story as a space for literary expression that offers something to the writer and reader that other forms do not.

One should note that DeLillo also publishes stories in small literary magazines such as the venerable *Granta,* as well as in small, obscure publications. His *Granta* stories have been published in special thematic issues of that magazine. The first story published there, "The Ivory Acrobat," (1994), appeared in a thematic issue with the title "Murder," edited by British writer Martin Amis. The biographical note about DeLillo contains the following sentence: "He [DeLillo] was living in Greece at the time of the 1981 earthquake."[8] "The Starveling" (2011), the second story he published in *Granta,* appeared in a special issue (devoted to the topic of "Horror") featuring writers such as Stephen King and Roberto Bolaño. DeLillo's stories in these two special issues resemble his public readings, where the relevance of what he reads on such occasions is often circumspect and original. In either case, the two stories in question take on different significance in the original context of publication. Like Edgar in "The Angel Esmeralda," these stories have biography and historical context after all; unlike hers, theirs is made privy to us.

In total, these seemingly disparate elements all point in one direction: to the way DeLillo writes. He described his working habits as follows in 1993: "When I was working on *The Names,* I devised a new method—new to me, anyway. When I finished a paragraph, even a three line paragraph, I automatically went to a fresh sheet of paper to start the new paragraph. No crowded pages. This enabled me to see a given set of sentences more clearly. It made rewriting easier and more effective. The white space on the page helped me concentrate more deeply on what I'd written."[9]

Readers who have attended DeLillo's public readings will have noted perhaps that he sometimes reads from a stack of typed pages, which he turns at irregular intervals. The audience sees it and the writer describes it, but the typed page vanishes into the consecutive paragraphs in the printed pages of books and magazines. DeLillo's modular working method suggests physical reasons for the compact organization of his literary prose, and particularly that of the period following *The Names,* the writings of which he clearly favors (the same being implicitly true of the later short fiction). One can also imagine the method extending to the interwoven narrative threads of *The Body Artist,* wherein the sentences of the opening chapter appear cut from two perspectives (those of Lauren and Rey), then reassembled into a single narrative, as if DeLillo had not written one paragraph but spliced one sentence per page only to later splice them into the published order.

By virtue of its brevity, however, the short story is not a form that would seem to nurture extensive experiments with narrative form within a single piece (although one might argue that DeLillo's recent shorter novels are his most technically accomplished in that regard). Critical readings of the matter are rare, however, a problem that is underscored by the economics of scholarly publishing. (Monograph-length studies of the short story are scarce, and increasingly so.) One might take the naïve view and argue that the short story speaks for itself and is therefore immune to elaborate critical evaluation. With respect to DeLillo, the lack of critical writings is surprising given the quality of the work in question. Of course, there is the matter of declining readerships to consider, too, as well as the ephemeral nature of the periodical: when the next issue is published, covers of the unsold copies are returned to the distributor and the remainder of each issue thrown away. Libraries, collectors, and the occasional second-hand shop offer sanctuary to what remains.

There exists nonetheless a rich history of humanistic inquiry in the study of the short story. As with the study of DeLillo's short fiction, such criticism is often embedded within longer studies on literary prose. One important modern example is that offered by Georg Lukács, who mused on the short story in *The Theory of the Novel* (1920) as follows: "In the short story, the narrative form which pinpoints the strangeness and ambiguity of life, such lyricism [as that of the minor epic form] must entirely conceal itself behind the hard outlines of the event. . . . The short story is the most purely artistic form: it expresses the ultimate meaning of all artistic creation as *mood*, as the very sense and content of the creative process."[10] One might note that Lukács has ignored here the technical innovations of Edgar Allan Poe, innovations that recalibrated the trajectory of much modern writing (and not only short fiction) by favoring the amorphous category of "mood."

Lukács's quasi-romantic emphasis remains true, however, insofar as it stresses the subjectivity of the form. That subjectivity had its precedent in the historical distinction between "sketch" and "tale," a division fundamental to understanding the development of literary fiction in the United States during the early nineteenth century. Jonathan Arac notes that the division is evident in the works of Washington Irving. In the sketch, Arac notes, "nothing happens . . . except for the verbal action of displaying to the reader something that the narrating voice considers of interest," whereas "in the tale something does happen, often something rather remarkable."[11] Arac goes on to note that the sketch is aligned with the first-person narrative voice, the tale with the third person. The distinction is rarely absolute in modern fiction; even Irving combined the sketch with the tale in "The Legend of Sleepy Hollow." The legend is narrated in the first person, but as we learn from the fictional historian Diedrich Knickerbocker's postscript, he heard it told at a public reading in New York City, from which he collected it (specifically referring to it as a "tale"). The postscript is itself in the manner of a sketch, told in the first person, describing the context of the tale's reading and a certain exchange between the storyteller (the implied narrator of the main tale) and a certain "cautious old gentleman," in which nothing is concluded but which leaves the reader wondering as to poor Ichabod's actual, as opposed to legendary, fate.

In narrative terms DeLillo's stories are often divided between the first-person manner of the sketch and the third-person narration of the tale. The story "The Runner" (1988), in which a jogger sees a kidnapping, most clearly resembles the sketch by virtue of its brevity and the protagonist's ambiguity regarding his initial reaction to one witness's explanation of the event and his later falsified explanation of it to that same witness. "The Angel Esmeralda" most closely resembles a descendant of the "tale," with its third-person voice, overt spiritualism, and detailed scrutiny of events. But DeLillo's stories also distort these admittedly arbitrary distinctions, and at times they do so by experimenting with narration and perspective. "Midnight in Dostoevsky" is DeLillo's story about two college students who imagine an elderly local man in their college town to be a spy defected or expelled (or perhaps not) from behind the Iron Curtain. The majority of the story, which is narrated in the pluralized first-person point of view ("we" is the story's favored pronoun), stresses a shared atmosphere and inference until the final confrontation, which in the end disrupts the pronoun's integrity. There is the intensely subjective first-person narration that typifies "The Starveling" and "Hammer and Sickle," the latter being perhaps DeLillo's most timely short story. It seems a microcosm, told from the point of view of an imprisoned father and financier, about the turbulent global capital markets after speculating banks destroyed them in 2008. "Hammer and Sickle" inhabits a terrain in between his earlier novel *Cosmopolis* (2003) and the ambiguous atmospheres of his short fiction, as a sketch in the form of a tale.

As noted earlier, critical analysis of DeLillo's short fiction is scarce. The major volumes of collected criticism edited by Harold Bloom (2003) and Frank Lentricchia (1991) seldom mention it, and most often in passing. When a critic turns attention to the short fiction, the strategy is generally the same: it is regarded in those instances as a precursor to the novels, a shorthand way of introducing some feature that will appear in grander form therein. For example, Tim Engles uses two early short stories "Take the 'A' Train" (1962) and "Spaghetti and Meatballs" (1965) in an essay on individualism, white masculinity, and identity in DeLillo's fiction. Stripping the stories of their ethnic context and language, Engles invokes Daniel Aaron's arguments that refute the import of DeLillo's Italian American roots as a key to understanding his works. Engles proceeds to disagree with Aaron's claim and argue that while

DeLillo's fiction stresses "individuals," it does not necessarily renounce group affiliation. Rather, its focus is critical in nature: DeLillo's characters complicate "the white authorial tendency to create autonomous, individual protagonists."[12] Josephine Gattuso Hendin uses the same two short stories to make a somewhat different case: that ethnicity, and in particular the renunciation of Italian American ethnicity, is a key feature of DeLillo's novel *Underworld*. Astutely using Antonio Gramsci's writings on *cultura negata* (or "negated folk culture") to explain the dynamic, Hendin argues that DeLillo's novel acts out a process of assimilation, a movement from "ethnicity" that typifies broader social movements of the postwar era, thereby resulting in another sort of group identity, one whose common ground is that of a lost, or self-negated, history whose traces are inscribed in the in the novel's descriptions of "found art."[13]

In these two examples, we see how biographical criticism remains a flashpoint, and an extraordinarily generative one at that, in discussions of DeLillo's fiction. In both cases, however, critics treat the short fiction as a passing curiosity, a sort of straw man that is used simultaneously to introduce an argument and to prefigure (even if by way of contrast) some later concern or feature of the novels. One finds this to be true even in discussions of later, "nonethnic" short fiction by DeLillo. With respect to the earlier fiction, a short story such as "The Uniforms" (1970) is used to prove DeLillo's interest in cinema and introduce a novel or novels.[14] Discussing a more recent story, DeLillo's "Baader-Meinhoff" (2002), Linda S. Kauffman has noted that the story itself shares in the post-9/11 problematics of DeLillo's New York fiction by drawing "parallels between German and American state repression [which] are never explicit, but never far from mind."[15] Kauffman's excellent explanation of the story admits that its connection to 9/11 "is difficult to pin down," a phrase that captures the difficulty that DeLillo's stories pose to readers who seek to compare them with his novels.

Mark Osteen's *American Magic and Dread* (2000) is comparable to Kauffman's essay by virtue of the subtlety, insight, and scope with which it treats the short fiction. Osteen's book contains one of the more extensive critical discussions of DeLillo's short fiction. The first half of its first chapter is devoted to analysis of DeLillo's early short fiction; occasional remarks on later stories appear in other sections. The book is also the most critical discussion of DeLillo's short fiction insofar as it recognizes the serious designs of the works. As other critics have done, Osteen claims that the stories prefigure elements of later novels. Discussing DeLillo's story "Coming Sun. Mon. Tues." (1966), Osteen notes that it contains "hyperarticulate characters [who] exchange mini essays in tersely elegant prose."[16] He discusses similarities between the novels and stories but also notes important differences in the manner in which DeLillo will engage the same topic in later novels. The most important feature of Osteen's argument is drawn from the film director Jean-Luc Godard, whose "essayistic" films he cites as a source of inspiration (as well as content, as the story alludes to them) for DeLillo's short stories. Continuing through extensive discussions of "Baghdad Towers West" (1968) and "The Uniforms" (1970), Osteen concludes that DeLillo's stories raise critical questions "exploring the collusion between cinema and consumerism, [whereby] DeLillo questions the possibility of any truly radical filmmaking aesthetic. And by hammering new frames around these pretextual films, DeLillo presents advertisements for the future that turn the camera back upon novelists and image makers, as if to ask, 'to what degree is our art just another consumer product?'"[17] In this way, Osteen usefully describes how DeLillo used short fiction to elaborate, and sometimes refute, ideas that would appear in his later novels.

Generally speaking, critics who have written about DeLillo's short fiction have focused on DeLillo's earliest stories. These works, all of which were presumably written in the 1960s (the last of them, "The Uniforms," was published in 1970), are generally privileged because critics claim that they offer "previews," as Osteen calls them, of DeLillo's later work. If we agree with Osteen's formidable arguments, we risk conceding that privilege and thereby diminishing DeLillo's talents as a writer of short fiction. As a result, we risk fusing the short fiction into the biographies of the novels in question. It is a sequence that erases precisely that which makes the stories unique: their mythic sense of time beyond time, what Trusller calls the "suspended" temporality of short fiction and what Boxall describes as the "unmeasured time" that would seem to carry over from the stories to DeLillo's more recent short novels.

Patterns of development and elaboration are evident in DeLillo's writings. Those patterns do extend from the stories to the novels, where at times they attain a more elaborate development in the latter form. As such, it is reasonable to regard DeLillo's short stories as playing a role in the development of the longer novels but not only to celebrate the novels at the expense of the short fiction. Critics might instead reconsider how we privilege the novel as the key by which we explain his career. Reconsidering the privilege does not require reversing its priority so as to afford new status to the short fiction. We might instead keep in mind that DeLillo's short stories and novels are distinct literary forms that travel in similar directions along parallel courses, the novels moving on a contemporaneous line, the stories in extemporaneous flight.

NOTES

Introduction

1. Arac, "Violence and the Human Voice," 55.

2. Begley, "The Art of Fiction CXXXV," 96.

3. Ibid., 93–94.

4. Knight, "DeLillo, Postmodernism, Postmodernity," 28.

5. Said, *On Late Style,* 7.

Chapter 1: Understanding Don DeLillo

1. Said, *Joseph Conrad and the Fiction of Autobiography,* 122. Italics appear in the original.

2. Burn, "Wired Up and Whacked Out," 38.

3. Ibid.

4. Pivano, *Amici Scrittori,* 114.

5. Bureau of the Census, *Sixteenth Census of the United States: 1940,* Department of Commerce, Bureau of the Census (Washington D.C., 1940). The specific document containing the DeLillo family's census information is available online as "Population Schedule, Pottsville City, PA, Sheet no. 12-A," National Archives and Records Administration, http://1940census.archives. gov/ (accessed May 17, 2013).

6. Talese, *Unto the Sons,* 4.

7. Begley, "The Art of Fiction CXXXV," 88.

8. Brecht, "Life Story of the Boxer Samson Körner," 207.

9. Aaron, "How to Read Don DeLillo," 67–68.

10. Lentricchia, "The American Writer as Bad Citizen," 1–6.

11. Gardaphé, *Italian Signs, American Streets,* 174.

12. Hungerford, "Don DeLillo's Latin Mass," 345, 352. DeLillo has occasionally discussed his Catholic upbringing in interviews. See also LeClair, "An Interview with Don DeLillo," 10.

13. Major writers in twentieth-century American letters who were baptized or raised in the Catholic Church include figures such as novelists Flannery O'Connor and Walker Percy, literary critics Allen Tate, F. O. Matthiessen, and Mary McCarthy, and poets Ted Berrigan and William Carlos Williams. I regard Ross Labrie's *The Catholic Imagination in American Literature* (1997) to be a representative study.

14. Basu, "Reading the Techno-Ethnic Other," 87–111.

15. For DeLillo's discussion of jazz music and museums, see Burn, "Wired Up and Whacked Out," 37–38. In addition to depicting New York baseball teams and their

environs in *Mao II* and *Underworld*, a quick internet search will turn up photographs of DeLillo in attendance at baseball games.

16. DeLillo, "Baader-Meinhof," in *The Angel Esmeralda*, 106.

17. DeLillo, "Hammer and Sickle," in *The Angel Esmeralda*, 175.

18. Critics have sometimes used Sontag's essay to frame discussion of these matters in DeLillo's novels. See Osteen, *American Magic and Dread*, 104–6. The most recent discussion appears in Olster, "*White Noise*," 84.

19. Osteen, "DeLillo's Dedalian Artists," 138.

20. Begley, "The Art of Fiction CXXXV," 88.

21. DeCurtis, "An Outsider in this Society," 67.

22. Camus, *The Fall*, 88.

23. DeCurtis, "An Outsider in this Society," 56, 73.

24. Lentricchia, "The American Writer as Bad Citizen," 3.

25. Two years after DeLillo received the award, Ralph Gardner Jr. published a related story in the *New York Times* describing how DeLillo codesigned a writing course for patients with Alzheimer' disease. See Gardner, "Writing That Can Strengthen the Fraying Threads of Memory." For more information on the Wallace Foundation, see http://www.wallacefoundation.org/Pages/default.aspx (accessed May 10, 2013).

26. Ruppersburg and Engles, "Introduction," 1.

Chapter 2: Jargon and Genre

1. Over the course of DeLillo's career, publishers have generally used the dust jackets, color schemes, and print layouts for American editions of DeLillo's books to convey an indirect sense of some feature or quality of the work. By contrast, the covers of Thomas Pynchon's novels lack this quality of design, while the dust jacket presentation of other authors—one might look at the "script letter" covers of recent editions of Toni Morrison's novels—suggest a carefully planned visual marketing strategy that grants a distinctive look to the author's books. (One might very well say the same for the paperback editions of DeLillo's fiction issued by Vintage during the 1990s or the British editions of DeLillo' recently published by Picador.)

2. Oates, "Young Man at the Brink of Self-Destruction," 5-E.

3. Cowart, "For Whom the Bell Tolls," 604.

4. As the novel concludes, David visits Dealey Plaza, the site of John F. Kennedy's assassination, a moment that critics regard as a preview of scenes in later DeLillo novels more thoroughly devoted to paranoia, politics, and history.

5. David Cowart warns against the temptation to reduce the book to autobiography, yet also claims that DeLillo is six years older than the narrator—a difference in age that is never entirely clear because of the narrator's conflicting references to dates. See Cowart, "For Whom the Bell Tolls," 604.

6. DiPietro, Introduction, ix.

7. See Cowart, "For Whom the Bell Tolls," 602–3.

8. Ibid.

9. Boxall, "DeLillo and Media Culture," 48.

10. Nel, "DeLillo and Modernism," 13. See also that essay's postmodern other, "DeLillo, Postmodernism, Postmodernity," in that same volume, wherein Peter Knight argues that "it is the explicitness with which DeLillo acknowledges his enormous debt to modernism that ends up rendering him postmodern" (27).

11. Lentricchia, "*Libra* as Postmodern Critique," 194.

12. Giaimo, Appreciating Don DeLillo, 57.
13. Aaron, "How to Read Don DeLillo," 69, 77.
14. LeClair, *In the Loop,* 98.
15. DeCurtis, "An Outsider in this Society," 57, 133.
16. McClure, "Postmodern Romance," 99.
17. Ibid., 102.
18. LeClair, in the Loop, 11.
19. LeClair, "An Interview with Don DeLillo," 5.
20. Dore, "The Rock Novel and Jonathan Lethem's *Fortress of Solitude.*"
21. Ibid.
22. LeClair, "An Interview with Don DeLillo," 6.
23. DeCurtis, "An Outsider in this Society," 65.
24. Ibid., 67.
25. DeCurtis, "'The Product,'" 131, 133.

Chapter 3: Opacity and Transparency

1. DeLillo, "Letter," 3–4.
2. Ferraro, "Whole Families Shopping at Night," 17.
3. Orr, *Don DeLillo's White Noise,* 21.
4. Bawer, "Don DeLillo's America," 24.
5. Ibid., 22.
6. Will, "Shallow Look at the Mind of an Assassin," 56.
7. Goodheart, "Don DeLillo and the Cinematic Real," 121.
8. See Connolly, "An Interview with Don DeLillo," 37.
9. See Osteen, *American Magic and Dread,* 8–10.
10. Begley, "The Art of Fiction CXXXV," 99.
11. Ibid., 93.
12. Arensberg, "Seven Seconds," 45.
13. Lentricchia, "The American Writer as Bad Citizen," 3.
14. Ibid., 2.
15. Ibid., 3.
16. Ibid., 3.
17. Ibid., 5.
18. Ibid., 2.
19. Aaron, "How to Read Don DeLillo," 76.
20. Ibid., 75.
21. LeClair, "An Interview with Don DeLillo," 8.
22. Begley, "The Art of Fiction CXXXV," 97.
23. Osteen, *American Magic and Dread,* 140.
24. Boxall, *Don DeLillo,* 187.
25. Cowart, "DeLillo and the Power of Language," 151.
26. See Weatherby, *Salman Rushdie,* 126–28. I refer to Weatherby's account for several reasons, including its excellent research in the later chapters (the early biographical chapters are not as strong), but I refer to it primarily because it was published prior to DeLillo's novel and may have been used as a source.
27. Ibid., 108. Edward W. Said published several articles about Rushdie, and Said's later writings refer occasionally to the matter.
28. Ibid., 189.

29. Nel, "DeLillo and Modernism," 24.
30. Nadotti, "An Interview with Don DeLillo," 112.
31. Barrett, "*Mao II* and Mixed Media," 54.
32. Adam Begley, "The Art of Fiction CXXXV," 10.
33. Weatherby, *Salman Rushdie,* 91–92. Weatherby interviewed Godwin for the book.
34. Knight, "*Mao II* and the New World Order," 42.
35. Barrett, "*Mao II* and Mixed Media," 62.
36. Boxall, "DeLillo and Media Culture," 44.
37. Ibid., 52.

Chapter 4: Artists and Prophets

1. Samuel Cohen offers a relevant sidelong glance at Fukuyama's arguments in his critical literary book *After the End of History* (129–30), a work that also includes an epilogue on DeLillo's *Underworld* and its anticipation of the alleged "post-historical" advent and impulse of the new millennium.
2. Steiner, "Look Who's Modern Now," 18–19.
3. Steiner, "The End of Traditionalism," 497. It should also be noted that Steiner's essay revisits the argument she made regarding Pynchon in the conclusion to her section of the *Cambridge History* but instead using DeLillo as the main example. For a more persuasive and thoughtful critique of DeLillo's *Underworld,* readers should consult Tony Tanner's "Don DeLillo and 'the American Mystery.'" Tanner explains how DeLillo's recent work had exaggerated the novelist's displacement by the terrorist, among other things.
4. Haworth-Booth, "Introduction," 15–24. The quoted words appear on page 23.
5. See Kessel, *Reading Landscape in American Literature* 144. While I use Kessel's quote to illustrate a critical point, I would disagree with Kessler's terminology insofar as I believe the gerund lacks subtlety or fails to note distinctions between "texts," or, for that matter, the reader's actively performative role vis-à-vis Lauren's character as well as the intonations of DeLillo's syntax.
6. Boxall, *Don DeLillo,* 220.
7. Gaiamo, *Appreciating Don DeLillo.* For quotes, see pages 162, 163, and 166.
8. Boxall, *Don DeLillo,* 215–17.
9. McClure, "Postmodern Romance," 102.
10. Gates, *Business @ the Speed of Thought,* 265.
11. Ibid., xvii.
12. Kunkel, "Dangerous Characters," 15.
13. Ibid., 14.
14. Kakutani, "A Man, A Woman, and a Day of Terror."
15. Bonca, "Contact with the Real."
16. Denby, "Creep Shows."
17. The former volume devotes two pages to a discussion of globalization in *Cosmopolis.* See Rowe, "Global Horizons in *Falling Man,*" 123–24.
18. McClure, "DeLillo and Mystery," 175.
19. Helyer, "DeLillo and Masculinity," 134–35.
20. Knight, "DeLillo, Postmodernism, Postmodernity," 35.
21. Conte, "Writing amid the Ruins," 179.
22. Ibid., 181.

23. Boxall, *Don DeLillo,* 221.
24. O'Hagan, "Don DeLillo Gets Under America's Skin," 8.
25. Kauffmann, "Bodies in Rest and Motion in *Falling Man,*" 135.
26. Apitzsch, "The Art of Terror—The Terror of Art," 96.
27. Ibid., 104.
28. Duvall, "Fiction and 9/11," 185.
29. Ibid.
30. Apitzsch, "The Art of Terror—The Terror of Art," 97.
31. Kauffmann, "Bodies in Rest and Motion in *Falling Man,*" 148.
32. Ibid., 151.
33. Kauffmann, "World Trauma Center," 655.
34. Pöhlmann, "Collapsing Identities," 51.
35. Kauffman, "The Wake of Terror," 21.
36. Salván, "Terror, Asceticism, and Epigrammatic Writing," 145.
37. Ibid., 153.
38. Ibid., 154.
39. See, for example, Bizzini, "Grieving and Memory in Don DeLillo's *Falling Man,*" 40–42.
40. Pöhlmann, "Collapsing Identities," 51.
41. Kauffman, "The Wake of Terror," 20.
42. Said, *On Late Style,* 6.
43. Ibid., 7.
44. Wagner-Martin, "The Twenty-First Century," 327.

Chapter 5: With, to, and against the Novel

1. Trussler, "Suspended Narratives," 558.
2. Ibid.
3. Ibid., 557.
4. Curt Gardner and Phil Nel have kept a running bibliography of DeLillo's publications at http://www.perival.com/delillo/ddbiblio.html (accessed March 19, 2013). Their list distinguishes clearly between "Stories" and "Short Fiction Excerpts," and it is a useful starting point for the reader who is interested in DeLillo's short fiction.
5. McClure, "DeLillo and Mystery," 174.
6. Denning, *Mechanic Accents,* 10.
7. Begley, "The Art of Fiction CXXXV," 93.
8. "Notes on Contributors," *Granta* 25 (Autumn 1988): 255.
9. Begley, "The Art of Fiction CXXXV," 92.
10. Lukács, *The Theory of the Novel,* 51.
11. Arac, *Emergence of American Literary Narrative,* 31.
12. Engles, "Who Are You, Literally?" 174–75.
13. Hendin, "*Underworld,* Ethnicity, and Found Object Art," 99.
14. Engles, "DeLillo and the Political Thriller," 68.
15. Kauffman, "The Wake of Terror," 27.
16. Osteen, *American Magic and Dread,* 9.
17. Ibid., 16.

BIBLIOGRAPHY

Primary Works

NOVELS

U.S. Editions

Americana. Boston: Houghton Mifflin, 1971.
End Zone. Boston: Houghton Mifflin, 1972.
Great Jones Street. Boston: Houghton Mifflin, 1973.
Ratner's Star. New York: Knopf, 1976.
Players. New York: Knopf, 1977.
Running Dog. New York: Knopf, 1978.
The Names. New York: Knopf, 1982.
White Noise. New York: Viking, 1985.
Libra. New York: Viking, 1988.
Mao II. New York: Viking, 1991.
Underworld. New York: Scribner, 1997.
The Body Artist. New York: Scribner, 2001.
Pafko at the Wall. New York: Scribner, 2001.
Cosmopolis. New York: Scribner, 2003.
Falling Man. New York: Scribner, 2007.
Point Omega. New York: Scribner, 2010.

U.K. Editions

Americana. Harmondsworth: Penguin, 1971.
End Zone. Harmondsworth: Penguin, 1972.
Great Jones Street. London: Picador, 1998
Ratner's Star. London: Vintage, 1991.
Players. London: Vintage, 1991.
Running Dog. London: Picador, 1999.
The Names. London: Picador, 1999.
White Noise. London: Picador, 1999.
Libra. Harmondsworth: Penguin, 1989.
Mao II. London: Vintage, 1992.
Underworld. London: Picador, 1999.
The Body Artist. London: Picador, 2000.

Cosmopolis. London: Picador, 2003.
Falling Man. London: Picador, 2007.
Point Omega. London: Picador, 2010.

MAJOR PLAYS

U.S. Editions

The Day Room. New York: Knopf, 1987.
Valparaiso. New York: Scribner, 1999.
Love-Lies-Bleeding. New York: Scribner, 2005.

U.K. Editions

The Day Room. London: Picador, 1999.
Valparaiso. London: Picador, 2004.
Love-Lies-Bleeding. London: Picador, 2006.

SCREENPLAY

Game 6. Directed by Michael Hoffman. Santa Monica, CA.: Serenade Films, 2005.

COLLECTED SHORT FICTION

The Angel Esmeralda. New York: Scribner, 2012; London: Picador, 2012.

UNCOLLECTED SHORT FICTION

"The River Jordan." *Epoch* 10.2 (1960): 105–20.
"Take the 'A' Train." *Epoch* 12.1 (1962): 9–25.
"Spaghetti and Meatballs." *Epoch* 14.3 (1965): 244–50.
"Coming Sun. Mon. Tues." *Kenyon Review* 28.3 (1966): 391–94.
"Baghdad Towers West." *Epoch* 17 (1968): 195–217.
"The Uniforms." *Carolina Quarterly* 22.1 (1970): 4–11.
"In the Men's Room of the Sixteenth Century." *Esquire,* December 1971, 174–77, 243, 246.

ESSAYS

"Towards a Definitive Meditation (By Someone Else) on the Novel *Americana*." *Epoch* 21.3 (1972): 327–29.
"Notes on 'The Uniforms.'" In *Cutting Edges: Young American Fiction for the '70's,* edited by Jack Hicks, 532–33. New York: Holt, Rinehart, and Winston, 1973.
"American Blood: A Journey through the Labyrinth of Dallas and JFK." *Rolling Stone,* December 8, 1983, 21–28, 74.
"Silhouette City: Hitler, Manson and the Millennium." *Dimensions: A Journal of Holocaust Studies* 4.3 (1988): 29–34.
Salman Rushdie Defense Pamphlet, by Don DeLillo and Paul Auster. New York: Rushdie Defense Committee USA, February 14, 1994.
"The Artist Naked in a Cage." *New Yorker,* May 26, 1997, 6–7.
"The Power of History." *New York Times Magazine,* September 7, 1997, 60–63.
"In the Ruins of the Future: Reflections on Terror and Loss in the Shadow of September." *Harper's,* December 2001, 33–40.
"Letter." In *White Noise,* translated by Zhu Ye, 3–4. Beijing: Yilin Press, 2002.

PERSONAL PAPERS

DeLillo, Don. Papers. The Henry Ransom Humanities Research Center. The University of Texas at Austin.

INTERVIEWS AND PROFILES

Arensberg, Ann. "Seven Seconds." In *Conversations with Don DeLillo,* edited by Thomas DiPietro, 40–46. Jackson, Miss.: University Press of Mississippi, 2005.

Bartholomew, Rafe. "Director's Cut: Q&A with Don DeLillo." *Grantland.com,* October 3, 2011. Accessed April 29, 2013. http://www.grantland.com/story/_/id/7032210/qa-don-delillo.

Begley, Adam. "The Art of Fiction CXXXV: Don DeLillo." In *Conversations with Don DeLillo,* edited by Thomas DiPietro, 86–108. Jackson, Miss.: University Press of Mississippi, 2005.

Burn, Gordon. "Wired Up and Whacked Out." (London) *Sunday Times,* August 25, 1991, 36–38.

Connolly, Kevin. "An Interview with Don DeLillo." In *Conversations with Don DeLillo,* edited by Thomas DiPietro, 25–39. Jackson, Miss: University Press of Mississippi, 2005.

DeCurtis, Anthony. "An Outsider in this Society." In *Conversations with Don DeLillo,* edited by Thomas DiPietro, 52–74. Jackson, Miss: University Press of Mississippi, 2005.

DiPietro, Thomas, ed. *Conversations with Don DeLillo.* Literary Conversations Series. Jackson: University Press of Mississippi, 2005.

Farkas, Allessandra. "DeLillo: Il lato oscuro dello Yankee." *Il Corriere della Sera,* May 13, 2002.

Gardner, Ralph, Jr. "Writing that Can Strengthen the Fraying Threads of Memory." *New York Times,* January 30, 1997.

Heron, Kim. "Haunted by His Book." *New York Times Book Review,* July 24, 1988, 23.

James, Caryn. "I Never Set Out to Write an Apocalyptic Novel." *New York Times Book Review,* January 13, 1985, 31.

Kamp, David. "DeLillo's Home Run." *Vanity Fair,* September 1997, 202–4.

LeClair, Thomas. "An Interview with Don DeLillo." In *Conversations with Don DeLillo,* edited by Thomas DiPietro, 3–15. Jackson, Miss.: University Press of Mississippi, 2005.

Nadotti, Maria. "An Interview with Don DeLillo." In *Conversations with Don DeLillo,* edited by Thomas DiPietro, 109–18. Jackson, Miss.: University Press of Mississippi, 2005.

Pivano, Fernanda. "Don DeLillo a New York: 1987." In *Amici Scrittori: Quarant' Anni di Incontri e Scoperte con gli Autori Americani,* 108–20. Milan: A. Mondadori, 1995.

Secondary Works

BOOKS

Arac, Jonathan. *The Emergence of American Literary Narrative, 1820–1860.* Cambridge, Mass.: Harvard University Press, 2005.

Bloom, Harold, ed. *Don DeLillo's* White Noise. Bloom's Modern Critical Interpretations. Broomall, Pa.: Chelsea House Publishers, 2003.

Boxall, Peter. *Don DeLillo: The Possibility of Fiction*. London: Routledge, 2006.

Camus, Albert. *The Fall*. Trans. Justin O'Brien. New York: Vintage Books: 1956.

Chodat, Robert. *Worldly Acts and Sentient Things: The Persistence of Agency from Stein to DeLillo*. Ithaca, N.Y.: Cornell University Press, 2008.

Cowart, David. *Don DeLillo: The Physics of Language*. Athens: University of Georgia Press, 2003.

Denning, Michael. *Mechanic Accents: Dime Novels and Working-Class Culture in America*. Rev. ed. New York: Verso, 1998.

Dewey, Joseph. *Beyond Grief and Nothing: A Reading of Don DeLillo*. Columbia: University of South Carolina Press, 2006.

Duvall, John N., ed. *The Cambridge Companion to Don DeLillo*. New York: Cambridge University Press, 2008.

———. *Don DeLillo's* Underworld: *A Reader's Guide*. New York: Continuum, 2002.

Giaimo, Paul. *Appreciating Don DeLillo: The Moral Force of a Writer's Work*. Santa Barbara, Calif.: Praeger, 2011.

Gardaphé, Fred L. *Italian Signs, American Streets: The Evolution of Italian American Narrative*. Durham, N.C.: Duke University Press, 1996.

Gates, Bill, with Collins Hemingway. *Business @ the Speed of Thought: Using a Digital Nervous System*. New York: Warner Books, 1999.

Hantke, Stephen. *Conspiracy and Paranoia in Contemporary American Fiction: The Works of Don DeLillo and Joseph McElroy*. Frankfurt: Peter Lang, 1994.

Kavadlo, Jesse. *Don DeLillo: Balance at the Edge of Belief*. New York: Peter Lang, 2004.

Keesey, Douglas. *Don DeLillo*. United States Authors Series. New York: Twayne, 1993.

Kessel, Tyler. *Reading Landscape in American Literature: The Outsider in the Fiction of Don DeLillo*. New York: Cambria Press, 2011.

Labrie, Ross. *The Catholic Imagination in American Literature*. Columbia: University of Missouri Press, 1997.

LeClair, Tom. *In the Loop: Don DeLillo and the Systems Novel*. Urbana: University of Illinois Press, 1987.

Lentricchia, Frank, ed. *Introducing Don DeLillo*. Durham, N.C.: Duke University Press, 1991. Reprint of special issue, *South Atlantic Quarterly* 89.2 (1990).

———, ed. *New Essays on* White Noise. New York: Cambridge University Press, 1991.

Lukács, Georg. *The Theory of the Novel: A Historico-Philosophical Essay on the Forms of Great Epic Literature*. Translated by Anna Bostock. Cambridge, Mass.: MIT Press, 1971.

Martucci, Elise. *The Environmental Unconscious in the Fiction of Don DeLillo*. New York: Routledge, 2007.

McClure, John. *Late Imperial Romance*. London: Verso 1994.

———. *Partial Faiths: Postsecular Fiction in the Age of Pynchon and Morrison*. Athens: University of Georgia Press, 2007.

Olster, Stacey, ed. *Don DeLillo:* Mao II, Underworld, Falling Man. Continuum Studies in Contemporary North American Fiction. New York: Continuum, 2011.

Orr, Leonard. *Don Delillo's* White Noise: *A Reader's Guide*. New York: Continuum, 2003.

Osteen, Mark, ed. White Noise: *Text and Criticism.* Viking Critical Library Series. New York: Viking, 1998.

———. *American Magic and Dread: Don DeLillo's Dialogue with Culture.* Philadelphia: University of Pennsylvania Press, 2000.

Said, Edward W. *Joseph Conrad and the Fiction of Autobiography.* Cambridge: Harvard University Press, 1966.

———. *On Late Style: Music and Literature against the Grain.* New York: Pantheon Books, 2006.

Schuster, Marc. *Don DeLillo, Jean Baudrillard, and the Consumer Conundrum.* Youngstown, NY: Cambria Press, 2008.

Talese, Gay. *Unto the Sons.* New York: Knopf, 1992.

Weatherby, William J. *Salman Rushdie: Sentenced to Death.* New York: Carroll and Graff, 1990.

Weinstein, Arnold. *Nobody's Home: Speech, Self, and Place in American Fiction from Hawthorne to DeLillo.* New York: Oxford University Press, 1993.

BOOK SECTIONS

Aaron, Daniel. "How to Read Don DeLillo." In *Introducing Don DeLillo,* edited by Frank Lentricchia, 67–82. Durham, N.C.: Duke University Press, 1991.

Apitzsch, Julia. "The Art of Terror—The Terror of Art: DeLillo's Still Life of 9/11, Giorgio Morandi, Gerhard Richter, and Performance Art." In *Terrorism, Media and the Ethics of Fiction: Transatlantic Perspectives on Don DeLillo,* edited by Peter Schneck and Phillipp Schweighauser, 93–108. New York: Continuum, 2010.

Barrett, Laura. "*Mao II* and Mixed Media." In *Don DeLillo:* Mao II, Underworld, Falling Man, edited by Stacey Olster, 49–67. New York: Continuum, 2011.

———. "Don DeLillo." In *The Cambridge Companion to American Fiction After 1945,* edited by John N. Duvall, 244–55. New York: Cambridge University Press, 2012.

Bawer, Bruce. "Don DeLillo's America." In *Don DeLillo,* edited by Harold Bloom, 21–28. Philadelphia: Chelsea House, 2003.

Bizzini, Silvia Caporale. "Grieving and Memory in Don DeLillo's *Falling Man.*" In *Terrorism, Media and the Ethics of Fiction: Transatlantic Perspectives on Don DeLillo,* edited by Peter Schneck and Phillipp Schweighauser, 40–50. New York: Continuum, 2010.

Brecht, Bertolt. "Life Story of the Boxer Samson Körner." In *Bertolt Brecht: Short Stories, 1921–1946,* edited by John Willett and Ralph Mannheim, 207–24. New York: Methuen, 1983.

Brooker, Peter. "Meet Me in Tompkins Square: Jay McInerney's *Brightness Falls* and Don DeLillo's *Mao II.*" In *New York Fictions: Modernity, Postmodernism, the New Modern,* 219–40. New York: Longman, 1996.

Boxall, Peter. "DeLillo and Media Culture." In *The Cambridge Companion to Don DeLillo,* edited by John N. Duvall, 43–52. New York: Cambridge University Press, 2008.

Coale, Samuel C. *Paradigms of Paranoia: The Culture of Conspiracy in Contemporary American Fiction.* Tuscaloosa: University of Alabama Press, 2005.

Cohen, Samuel S. "Don DeLillo and the Anticipation of Retrospection." In *After the End of History: American Fiction in the 1990s,* 189–202. Iowa City: University of Iowa Press, 2009.

Conte, Joseph M. "Writing amid the Ruins: 9/11 and *Cosmopolis*." In *The Cambridge Companion to Don DeLillo*, edited by John N. Duvall, 179–92. New York: Cambridge University Press, 2008.

Cowart, David. "DeLillo and the Power of Language." In *The Cambridge Companion to Don DeLillo*, edited by John N. Duvall, 151–65. New York: Cambridge University Press, 2008.

DeCurtis, Anthony. "'The Product': Bucky Wunderlick, Rock 'n' Roll, and Don DeLillo's *Great Jones Street*." In *Introducing Don DeLillo*, edited by Frank Lentricchia, 131–42. Durham, N.C.: Duke University Press, 1991.

DiPietro, Thomas. Introduction. *Conversations with Don DeLillo*, edited by Thomas DiPietro, vii–xii. Jackson, Miss: University Press of Mississippi, 2005.

Duvall, John N. "Excavating the Underworld of Race and Waste in Cold War History: Baseball, Aesthetics, and Ideology." In *Critical Essays on Don DeLillo*, edited by Hugh Ruppersburg and Tim Engles, 259–81. New York: G. K. Hall, 2000.

———. "Fiction and 9/11." In *The Cambridge Companion to American Fiction after 1945*, edited by John N. Duvall, 181–92. New York: Cambridge University Press, 2012.

Eaton, Mark. "Inventing Hope: The Question of Belief in Don DeLillo's Novels." In *The Gift of Story: Narrating Hope in a Postmodern World*, edited by Mark Eaton, 31–49. Waco, Tex.: Baylor University Press, 2006.

Engles, Tim. "Who Are You, Literally?" In *Critical Essays on Don DeLillo*, edited by Hugh Ruppersburg and Tim Engles, 171–95. New York: G. K. Hall, 2000.

———. "DeLillo and the Political Thriller." In *The Cambridge Companion to Don DeLillo*, edited by John N. Duvall, 66–76. New York: Cambridge University Press, 2008.

Ferraro, Thomas J. "Whole Families Shopping at Night!" In *New Essays on* White Noise, edited by Frank Lentricchia, 15–38. Durham: Duke University Press, 1991.

Goodheart, Eugene. "Don DeLillo and the Cinematic Real." In *Introducing Don DeLillo*, edited by Frank Lentricchia, 117–30. Durham, N.C.: Duke University Press, 1991.

Green-Lewis, Jennifer, and Margaret Soltan. "Beauty after 9/11: Don DeLillo in New York." In *Teaching Beauty in DeLillo, Woolf, and Merrill*, 113–28. New York: Palgrave Macmillan, 2008.

Haworth-Booth, Mark. Introduction. *Shadow of Light: Photographs by Bill Brandt*, 15–24. DaCapo Press: New York, 1977.

Helyer, Ruth. "DeLillo and Masculinity." In *The Cambridge Companion to Don DeLillo*, edited by John N. Duvall, 125–36. New York: Cambridge University Press, 2008.

Hendin, Josephine Gattuso. "*Underworld*, Ethnicity, and Found Object Art: Reason and Revelation." In *Don DeLillo:* Mao II, Underworld, Falling Man, edited by Stacey Olster, 99–115. New York: Continuum, 2011.

Kauffmann, Linda S. "Bodies in Rest and Motion in *Falling Man*." In *Don DeLillo:* Mao II, Underworld, Falling Man, edited by Stacey Olster, 135–51. New York: Continuum, 2011.

———. "The Wake of Terror: Don DeLillo's 'In the Ruins of the Future,' 'Baader-Meinhof,' and *Falling Man*." In *Terrorism, Media and the Ethics of Fiction: Transatlantic Perspectives on Don DeLillo*, edited by Peter Schneck and Phillipp Schweighauser, 19–39. New York: Continuum, 2010.

Keener, John F. "Conspiratorial Identity: Biography, Fiction and the Oswald Enigma." In *Biography and the Postmodern Historical Novel*, 67–108. Lewiston: Edwin Mellen Press, 2001.

Knight, Peter. "DeLillo, Postmodernism, Postmodernity." In *The Cambridge Companion to Don DeLillo*, edited by John N. Duvall, 27–40. New York: Cambridge University Press, 2008.

———. "*Mao II* and the New World Order," In *Don DeLillo:* Mao II, Underworld, Falling Man, edited by Stacey Olster, 34–48. New York: Continuum, 2011.

Kuehl, John. *Alternate Worlds: A Study of Postmodern Antirealistic American Fiction.* New York: New York University Press, 1989.

Lentricchia, Frank. "The American Writer as Bad Citizen." In *Introducing Don DeLillo*, edited by Frank Lentricchia, 1–6. Durham, N.C.: Duke University Press, 1991.

———. "*Libra* as Postmodern Critique." In *Introducing Don DeLillo*, edited by Frank Lentricchia, 193–215. Durham, N.C.: Duke University Press, 1991.

McClure, John. "Postmodern Romance: Don DeLillo and the Age of Conspiracy." In *Introducing Don DeLillo*, edited by Frank Lentricchia, 99–116. Durham, N.C.: Duke University Press, 1991.

———. "DeLillo and Mystery." In *The Cambridge Companion to Don DeLillo*, edited by John N. Duvall, 166–78. New York: Cambridge University Press, 2008.

Mottram, Eric. "The Real Needs of Man: Don DeLillo's Novels." In *The New American Writing: Essays on American Literature Since 1970*, edited by Graham Clarke, 51–98. New York: St. Martin's Press, 1990.

Mullen, Bill. "No There There: Cultural Criticism as Lost Object in Don DeLillo's *Players* and *Running Dog*." In *Powerless Fictions? Ethics, Cultural Critique, and American Fiction in the Age of Postmodernism*, edited by Ricardo Miguel Alfonso, 113–40. Atlanta: Editions Rodopi B.V., 1996.

Nel, Philip. "DeLillo and Modernism." In *The Cambridge Companion to Don DeLillo*, edited by John N. Duvall, 13–26. New York: Cambridge University Press, 2008.

Olster, Stacey. "*White Noise*." In *The Cambridge Companion to Don DeLillo*, edited by John N. Duvall, 79–93. New York: Cambridge University Press, 2008.

Osteen, Mark. "DeLillo's Dedalian Artists." In *The Cambridge Companion to Don DeLillo*, edited by John N. Duvall, 137–50. New York: Cambridge University Press, 2008.

Pöhlmann, Sascha. "Collapsing Identities: The Representation and Imagination of the Terrorist in *Falling Man*." In *Terrorism, Media, and the Ethics of Fiction: Transatlantic Perspectives on Don DeLillo*, edited by Peter Schneck and Phillipp Schweighauser, 51–66. New York: Continuum, 2010.

Rowe, John Carlos. "Global Horizons in *Falling Man*." In *Don DeLillo:* Mao II, Underworld, Falling Man, edited by Stacey Olster, 121–34. New York: Continuum, 2011.

Ruppersburg, Hugh, and Tim Engles. Introduction. *Critical Essays on Don DeLillo*, edited by Hugh Ruppersburg and Tim Engles, 1–27. New York: G. K. Hall, 2000.

Salván, Paula Martín. "Terror, Asceticism, and Epigrammatic Writing in Don DeLillo's Fiction." In *Terrorism, Media and the Ethics of Fiction: Transatlantic Perspectives on Don DeLillo*, edited by Peter Schneck and Phillipp Schweighauser, 145–57. New York: Continuum, 2010.

Simmons, Phillip. "Don DeLillo's Invisible Histories." In *Deep Surfaces: Mass Culture and History in Postmodern American Fiction,* 41–82. Athens: University of Georgia Press, 1997.

Steiner, Wendy. "The End of Traditionalism." In *The Cambridge History of American Literature: Prose Writing (1940–1990),* edited by Sacvan Bercovitch, 479–98. Cambridge, U.K.: Cambridge University Press, 1994.

Tabbi, Joseph. "From the Sublime to the Beautiful to the Political: Don DeLillo at Midcareer." In *Postmodern Sublime: Technology and American Writing from Mailer to Cyberpunk,* 169–207. Ithaca: Cornell University Press, 1995.

Tanner, Tony. "Don DeLillo and 'the American Mystery': *Underworld.*" In *The American Mystery: American Literature from Emerson to DeLillo,* 201–21. New York: Cambridge University Press, 2000.

Wagner-Martin, Linda. "The Twenty-First Century." In *A History of American Literature, 1950–Present,* Wiley-Blackwell Histories of American Literature, edited by Alfred Bendixen and Richard Gray, 277–352. Malden, Mass.: Wiley-Blackwell, 2013.

Will, George F. "Shallow Look at the Mind of an Assassin." In *Critical Essays on Don DeLillo,* edited by Hugh Ruppersburg and Tim Engles, 56–57. New York: G. K. Hall, 2000.

ARTICLES

Arac, Jonathan. "Violence and the Human Voice: Critique and Hope in *Native Speaker,*" *boundary 2* 36.2 (2009): 55–66.

Baelo-Allué, Sonia. "9/11 and the Psychic Trauma Novel: Don DeLillo's *Falling Man.*" *ATLANTIS: Journal of the Spanish Association of Anglo-American Studies* 34.1 (2012): 63–79.

Barrett, Laura. "Here but Also There: Subjectivity and Postmodern Space in *Mao II.*" *Modern Fiction Studies* 45.3 (1999): 788–810.

Basu, Biman. "Reading the Techno-Ethnic Other in Don DeLillo's *White Noise.*" *Arizona Quarterly: A Journal of American Literature, Culture, and Theory* 61.2 (2005): 87–111.

Cowart, David. "For Whom the Bell Tolls: Don DeLillo's *Americana.*" *Contemporary Literature* 37.4 (1996): 602–19.

Deardorff, Donald L. "Dancing in the End Zone: Don DeLillo, Men's Studies, and the Quest for Linguistic Healing." *Journal of Men's Studies* 8.1 (1999): 73–82.

Dore, Florence. "The Rock Novel and Jonathan Lethem's *Fortress of Solitude.*" *Nonsite .org,* no. 8 (January 20, 2013). Accessed March 15, 2013. http://nonsite.org/article/the-rock-novel-and-jonathan-lethems-the-fortress-of-solitude.

Duvall, John N. "The (Super) Marketplace of Images: Television as Unmediated Mediation in DeLillo's *White Noise.*" *Arizona Quarterly* 3 (1994): 127–53.

Gardner, Ralph Jr. "Writing That Can Strengthen the Fraying Threads of Memory." *New York Times,* January 30, 1997, C1.

Hungerford, Amy. "Don DeLillo's Latin Mass." *Contemporary Literature* 47.1 (2006): 343–80.

Kauffman, Linda. "The Wake of Terror: Don Delillo's 'In The Ruins of The Future,' 'Baader-Meinhof,' and *Falling Man.*" *Modern Fiction Studies* 54.2 (2008): 353–77.

———. "World Trauma Center." *American Literary History* 21.3 (2009): 647–59.

Karnicky, Jeffrey. "Avian Consciousness in Don DeLillo's *The Body Artist.*"

Anthrozoos: A Multidisciplinary Journal of the Interactions of People and Animals 22: 1 (2009): 5–18.

Kunkel, Benjamin. "Dangerous Characters," *New York Times Book Review,* September 11, 2005.

Laist, Randy. "Apocalyptic Nostalgia in the Prologue of Don DeLillos *Underworld.*" *University of Edinburgh Postgraduate Journal of Culture and the Arts* (2010). Accessed December 10, 2012. http://www.forumjournal.org/site/issue/05/randy-laist.

Landon, Richard. "Sport Fiction and the Untellable: Cliché and Language in Don DeLillo's *End Zone.*" *Aethlon* 23.1 (2005): 71–80. Accessed March 10, 2013. http://www.la84foundation.org/SportsLibrary/Aethlon/2005/AethlonXXIII1/aethlonXXIIIr.pdf/

LeClair, Thomas. "Deconstructing the Logos: Don DeLillo's *End Zone.*" *Modern Fiction Studies* 33.1 (1987): 105–22.

Maltby, Paul. "The Romantic Metaphysics of Don DeLillo." *Contemporary Literature* 37.1 (1996): 258–77.

Mauro, Aaron. "The Languishing of the Falling Man: Don DeLillo and Jonathan Safran Foer's Photographic History of 9/11." *Modern Fiction Studies* 57.3 (2011): 584–606.

McClure, John. "Postmodern/Post-secular: Contemporary Fiction and Spirituality." *Modern Fiction Studies* 41 (1995): 141–63.

Moran, Joe. "Don DeLillo and the Myth of the Author-Recluse." *Journal of American Studies* 34.1 (April 2000): 137–52.

Osteen, Mark. "Becoming Incorporated: Spectacular Authorship and DeLillo's *Mao II.*" *Modern Fiction Studies* 45.3 (1999): 643–74.

Packer, Matthew J. "'At the Dead Center of Things' in Don DeLillo's *White Noise:* Mimesis, Violence, and Religious Awe." *Modern Fiction Studies* 51 (2005): 648–66.

Rowe, John Carlos. "*Mao II* and the War on Terror." *South Atlantic Quarterly* 103 (2004): 21–34.

Steiner, Wendy. "Look Who's Modern Now." *New York Times Book Review,* October 10, 1999.

Thomas, Glen. "History, Biography and Narrative in DeLillo's *Libra.*" *Twentieth Century Literature* 43.1 (1997): 107–24.

Trussler, Michael. "Suspended Narratives: The Short Story and Temporality." *Studies in Short Fiction* 33 (1996): 557–77.

REVIEWS

Algren, Nelson. "A Waugh in Shoulder Padding." Review of *End Zone* by Don DeLillo. In *Critical Essays on Don DeLillo,* edited by Hugh Ruppersburg and Tim Engles, 34–36. New York: G. K. Hall, 2000.

Bonca, Cornel. "Contact with the Real." Review of David Cronenberg's Film Adaptation of Don DeLillo's *Cosmopolis. Los Angeles Review of Books.* September 12, 2012.

Denby, David. "Creep Shows." Review of David Cronenberg's Film Adaptation of Don DeLillo's *Cosmopolis. New Yorker,* August 27, 2012. Accessed February 27, 2014. http://www.newyorker.com/arts/critics/cinema/2012/08/27/120827crci_cinema_denby.

Echlin, Kim. "Baseball and the Cold War." *Ottawa Citizen,* December 28, 1997, E5.

Kakutani, Michiko. "A Man, a Woman, and a Day of Terror." Review of *Falling Man* by Don DeLillo. *New York Times,* May 9, 2007. Accessed February 25, 2014. http://www.nytimes.com/2007/05/09/books/09kaku.html?pagewanted=all&_r=0.

Lehmann-Haupt, Christopher. "A Touchdown for Don DeLillo." Review of *End Zone* by Don DeLillo. *New York Times,* March 22, 1972. Accessed September 20, 2012. http://www.nytimes.com/books/97/03/16/lifetimes/del-r-endzone.html.

Oates, Joyce Carol. "Young Man at the Brink of Self-Destruction." Review of *Americana* by Don DeLillo. *Detroit News,* June 27, 1971: 5-E.

O'Hagan, Andrew. "Don DeLillo Gets under America's Skin." Review of *Underworld* by Don DeLillo. *Voice Literary Supplement,* Fall 1997.

Verso, Tom. "Don DeLillo Comes Home: 'Game 6' and 'Underworld.'" *i-Italy Magazine* 7, April 2008. Accessed April 25, 2013. http://www.i-italy.org/1588/don-delillo-comes-home-game-6-and-underworld.

Yardley, Jonathan. "The Co-authors of 'Amazons' Used a Pseudonym: To Avoid Red Faces?" *Sports Illustrated,* October 20, 1980. Accessed April 25, 2013. http://sportsillustrated.cnn.com/vault/article/magazine/MAG1123867/index.htm.

INDEX

ABOUT THE AUTHOR

HENRY VEGGIAN is a lecturer of English and comparative literature at the University of North Carolina at Chapel Hill. He edits for *boundary 2* and Rodopi Editions.